Becoming
Duchess
Goldblatt

Named one of the *New York Times* "20 Books We're
Watching For in 2020"

Named a "Most Anticipated Book of 2020" by
Real Simple and *The Millions*

A "Best Book of July" in the *New York Times,* Amazon, the
Christian Science Monitor, and Apple

An Indie Next Pick

A Best Book of the Summer from
Marie Claire, Iowa Public Radio, and *Boston*

"Deeply satisfying, unexpectedly moving . . . As lovable as the
duchess herself . . . In Duchess Goldblatt's digital neighborhood, people are not just welcome but completely adored . . .
Duchess and Anonymous subtly, slowly become one person.
She no longer feels alone; neither do her subjects. People find
solace in this fictional character — and Anonymous does,
too."

— **Julie Klam,** ***New York Times Book Review***

"After reading this unforgettable memoir, I figured out who Duchess Goldblatt is: all of us. Behind her brilliantly witty and uplifting message is a remarkable vulnerability and candor that reminds us that we are not alone in our struggles — and that we can, against all odds, get through them. As though casting a magic spell on her readers, she moves, inspires, and connects us through her unvarnished humanity. It was, for this therapist, a form of therapy I didn't know I needed."

— **Lori Gottlieb, *New York Times* best-selling author of *Maybe You Should Talk to Someone***

"There's no recipe for Duchess Goldblatt tweets, but they often amount to one part conventional wisdom and two parts surrealism, with some grandmotherly tenderness or saltiness sprinkled in for good measure . . . Her feed is one of the few places on the internet devoted to spreading unadulterated joy. It's also a successful example of social media literature, due in part to Duchess's voice, which requires readers to confront the ridiculousness of the entire premise alongside the sincerity of her musings . . . *Becoming Duchess Goldblatt* recontextualizes the Twitter account as a therapeutic exercise."

— **Kate Dwyer, *New York Times***

"This book is, like Duchess Goldblatt herself, nothing you expect and everything you need. It's a memoir not just of one life (failures and triumphs laid bare) but also of a second self — its creation, its evolution, its improbable splendor. We may never deserve Duchess Goldblatt and her magnanimity, but her inventor most certainly does."

— **Rebecca Makkai, author of the Pulitzer Prize and National Book Award finalist *The Great Believers***

"Uplifting."   — ***People,* "The Best New Books"**

"What an unexpected marvel of a book, funny and poignant and — dare I say — sweet. It's fashionable to bash social media, but without it, we wouldn't have Duchess and that would be a damn shame." — Laura Lippman, *New York Times* best-selling author of *Lady in the Lake* and *Sunburn*

"A tonic, a gift for our anxious summer . . . *Becoming Duchess Goldblatt* is many things, all of them splendid . . . The best sort of self-help, demonstrating that creativity, generosity, and even Twitter . . . can offer salvation and lift all boats . . . Anonymity liberates the author to share her story without restraint. The book is enriched by two distinct voices: one frank and vulnerable, the other all-knowing. You believe the details of the author's life because, though Duchess, she's committed to staying generous and true . . . This sort of anonymity, in a time of too much oversharing on too many platforms, is a respite. We need magic. The book's timing is inspired. It's a summer cocktail of a book. Of Duchess Goldblatt, we would expect nothing less." — *Washington Post*

"The question I am most often asked by readers out in the world is, 'Who is Duchess Goldblatt?' The correct answer is, 'She is the Universe's secret admirer, a made-up and hilarious octogenarian who lives on Twitter, who delivers love and demands it in equal, astonishing measure.' What they mean is: What's her real identity? This book does not precisely reveal that. Instead, it's the actual memoir of a fictional person, a meditation on what it means to start again in the oddest way possible. It is also heartbreaking, funny, gorgeously written, surprising, brilliant, profound, the book only Duchess Goldblatt herself could have written." — Elizabeth McCracken, best-selling author of *Bowlaway* and *The Giant's House*

"The writer goes to great lengths in the book to demarcate herself from the Duchess. Goldblatt is an alter ego, someone onto whom she can project her pain and have it come back in the form of jokes. An obvious model is Dorothy Parker, but in a way the writer's creative nimbleness and insistence on anonymity brings to mind someone more like Lee Israel . . . Her proclamations sound like pithy lines from a standup special — that is, if the comedian was God and if God was an eighty-one-year-old woman from the seventeenth century . . . What's most astonishing is the relationship Duchess has with her community . . . They find her amusing, comforting, assuring . . . Originally used as a tool to deal with her own trauma, over time the Duchess has mutated into something more like a movement. Duchess Goldblatt is a kind of way to rewrite the ways we treat ourselves and the people around us. The writer admits to a very famous friend she meets at one point in the book that the Duchess 'whispers' little prayers to each of her followers . . . It's loving the bizarre and cherishing the weird that Goldblatt does best. And it's why so many people trust her to tell them how to live, how to treat themselves with more compassion, how to treat each other better, too."

— *Boston Globe*

"A memoir that is, ironically, about the power a fiction can exert on us all, she tells us a story about late capitalism, social media, the financial crisis, and America, and being a woman trying to survive it all. Whatever someone expects this to be, it isn't, and that is, perhaps, the real secret to the Duchess underneath it all."

— **Alexander Chee, best-selling author of *The Queen of the Night* and *How to Write an Autobiographical Novel***

"The Duchess is a light shining in the darkness, a beacon for troubled souls scrolling through their phones in the wee hours of the morning. Her presence has uplifted her human avatar, even as it heartens Her Grace's ever-growing audience of 'loons' and 'rascals.' She might be an invention of social media, but — as the Duchess would say — her love is real."

— *BookPage*

"*Becoming Duchess Goldblatt* is a story about the importance of community — of kindness, acceptance, and friendship. The world would be a better place if we all became Duchess Goldblatt."

— **Lyle Lovett**

"A life-affirming memoir packed with hilarity and candid observations about life and love."

— *Marie Claire*

"A source of wry wisdom and off-kilter commentary . . . A testament to the powers of redemption, reinvention, and yes, country singer Lyle Lovett."

— *Christian Science Monitor*

"The fragmented nature of the internet lends itself to an aphoristic quality, and its anonymity has resurrected a certain *Respublica literaria* that can, for all of the web's reputation, feel downright Enlightenment. The anonymous woman behind the popular Duchess Goldblatt account on Twitter, with her avatar drawn from a Netherlands Renaissance portrait, is a case in point . . . Duchess Goldblatt has self-fashioned a persona delivering bon mots both witty and gnomic, all while using the internet itself as an aesthetic medium where the product is constructed identity . . . This anonymous memoir delivers."

— *The Millions*

Becoming
Duchess
Goldblatt

Becoming
Duchess
Goldblatt

ANONYMOUS

MARINER BOOKS · HOUGHTON MIFFLIN HARCOURT
Boston · New York

First Mariner Books edition 2021

Library of Congress Cataloging-in-Publication Data
Title: Becoming Duchess Goldblatt / Anonymous.
Description: Boston : Houghton Mifflin Harcourt, 2020.
Identifiers: LCCN 2019027260 (print) | LCCN 2019027261 (ebook) |
ISBN 9780358216773 (hardcover) | ISBN 9780358216797 (ebook) |
ISBN 9780358309376 | ISBN 9780358309451 | ISBN 9780358569831 (trade paper)
Subjects: LCSH: American wit and humor. | Conduct of life — Humor.
Classification: LCC PN6165 .D83 2020 (print) | LCC PN6165 (ebook) |
DDC 818/.602 [B] — dc23
LC record available at https://lccn.loc.gov/2019027260
LC ebook record available at https://lccn.loc.gov/2019027261

Book design by Chrissy Kurpeski

Printed in the United States of America
DOC 10 9 8 7 6 5 4 3 2 1

Wallace Stevens's definition of poetry is from "Of Modern Poetry,"
in *Collected Poems*. Used by permission of Faber and Faber Ltd.

For M.

Quit hounding me, children.
You don't need to know everything.

Becoming
Duchess
Goldblatt

1

꙰

I must have slept weird, folks. My backstory is killing me.

WHEN THE HOUSE burns down, so to speak, there's no guarantee that anybody will stick around to help sweep up. This is not the dominant narrative I'd been raised to believe in. Sure, Lucy and Ricky could end up divorced — the twin beds were a clue, in hindsight, and he was such a fascist about kicking her out of his stupid nightclub act — but you figure Lucy would always have Ethel Mertz. In my moment of sudden destruction, I learned the very hard way that reinforcements would not be coming. When I lost everything — my Ricky, my Fred and Ethel, the nightclub and band, even the gig on the chocolate-factory assembly line — I found out the sheltering trees above me were gone, and I was on my own.

It's Opening Day in Crooked Path! Looks like another beautiful season of head games, everybody.

I almost drove the car off the road when I saw the caller's name appear on my phone: Frank Delaney. I'd met the Irish writer maybe a year or two earlier, through work, and we'd hit it off, but I never would have expected him to call me up again out of the blue. Frank was a novelist and BBC journalist, and smooth — indeed, he'd been called "the most eloquent man in the world" by NPR — but I was struck again by how kind he was, how genuine, how compassionate. After we'd met just that one time, he'd sent along a gift for my little boy: a copy of Kaufman's *Field Guide to Butterflies of North America.*

Frank had a sharp eye and a storyteller's ear. He had interviewed thousands of people in his decades in broadcasting, everyone from Prince Charles to Alan Greenspan, and that expertise revealed itself: somehow in our short time together, over a day or two, he'd gotten my whole story out of me. I still don't know how he did it, how he ever perceived so much, so fast.

"How are you?" he asked me. "Are you all right? I hope by now you've stopped pushing people away."

I pulled the car off the road into an empty church parking lot. "I'm trying, Frank," I said. "Thanks for asking."

"What days are the hardest for you?" he asked.

"Sundays."

"So I'll tell you what you do on Sundays: French lessons. Dance lessons. Piano lessons. Immerse yourself in the deep pleasures of Latin and Greek. Sign yourself up for something every hour. Fill your days."

"Okay," I said. "Thank you."

"It will get easier with time," Frank said.

"All right."

"How's your son now?" he asked.

"You're so kind to ask. He's eight already, if you can believe it." I could hear my voice was shaky. "We're trying. We'll be okay."

"When you have no one to put their arms around you, you must put your arms around yourself," Frank Delaney said. "Will you do that?"

"I'll try, Frank," I said.

But I didn't know how.

> I'm looking for something shiny to show you in this garbage pile, loons. Maybe a bit of sea glass. I'm trying.

I can remember one day, during this period, hanging around at my job with nothing in particular to do. I worked as a writer and editor for a publishing house that had been started decades earlier by academics, and our beloved locally owned firm had recently been bought by a foreign company to be stripped down for parts. Four hundred or so of my colleagues had been let go. The handful of us who were allowed to stay on a little longer had a few projects to finish up here and there, if we cared to, and we did. We wanted to at least complete the work we'd started. Our lease wasn't quite up yet, so we stuck around, a few loose marbles rattling in an otherwise empty building. Desks and chairs were stacked floor to ceiling, and boxes of unwanted papers had been dumped in darkened conference rooms.

I went wandering the halls looking for coffee in the break room one day and ran into one of the guys from the new parent company. We both stood there silently waiting for the coffee to finish brewing until, finally, he cleared his throat.

"You know, usually when we go into an organization like this to clean it out, we start looking into the business and find out the place was a disaster, bleeding money," he said. "Mismanaged, driven into the ground. But this place" — he shook his head — "this was an American tragedy. It was a beautiful organization. Very, very well run. Solid margins. People cared. I mean, they really cared." He sounded surprised. I didn't give him the satisfaction of telling him he was right. It had been a beautiful organization. Of course we had cared. I held his gaze in silence until he turned and left the room.

The few of us who'd been lucky enough to have been kept around for a bit knew it wouldn't last. We all had to find new jobs. Most of our clients had split as soon as they saw the ship taking on water, and the little bit of work that was left for us didn't fill the whole day. In the meantime, we kept turning up every morning, mostly to have someplace to go.

"Show me how to set up an account on social media," I said to my work pal Naomi one day, in boredom. I was lying down on the desk in her office, staring at the ceiling. "I've never been on there. I feel like I'm missing out."

"You're not missing anything," she said. "It's all the people you haven't seen since high school posting pictures of their kids. Lot of libertarians with government jobs complaining about paying their taxes, for some reason."

"I wouldn't mind seeing what people are up to," I said. "As long as they can't see me."

"If you're out there, they can see you," she said. "It's reciprocal. That's the whole point. It's why they call it *social* media."

"And yet somehow I'm feeling like this is not the time for me to establish a public presence out amongst the people," I said, waving my hand in the direction of the hallway, by which I meant the street outside, our town, the world. She nodded.

Naomi knew enough of the salient details of my story that she supported my intuition not to start posting anything personal online at that very moment. She and I had both learned the hard way that family court judges and divorce attorneys are not typically the first to leap forth in an embrace of harmless good fun.

"Could you set up an account for me so I'm anonymous?" I asked.

"Anonymous?" she said. "You mean fake?"

"No. I can't lie. I certainly don't want to trick anybody," I said. "I'm thinking it could be obviously fictional. I'll use a pseudonym. I won't even post. I'll just listen in on what everyone else is saying."

"What's your pen name?" she said.

I thought about it. "You know that classic parlor game that lets you figure out your drag queen name? You take the name of the first pet you ever had as your first name and your mother's maiden name as your last name."

"I thought it was your first gym teacher's name and the name of the street you grew up on."

"That's a perversion of the form in my opinion, but yes. That's pretty much it."

"You can't use your own mother's maiden name," she said. "People who know you might recognize it."

"Good point. I won't use my own. What's your mother's maiden name?"

"Didion."

"Derivative," I snorted.

"Too bad. I'm not letting you use my mother's real maiden name. Keep looking."

"Fine. I'll tell you the funniest one I ever heard," I said. "A dear old friend of mine: his first dog was a black Lab named Duchess, and his mother's maiden name was Goldblatt."

"Duchess Goldblatt."

"I've always loved it. It's so fun to say. And it sounds made-up, so I think people would take the hint right away that this is not a real person."

"All right, so then you'll need a picture to go with the name."

I liked the idea of a person who was real but not real, so I searched on the term "funny elderly lady."

"These are all the wrong vibe. They're so corny," I said. "I want people to get a visual cue right away that this is a fictional character."

I changed the search terms to "elderly lady."

One of the first images to come up then was an oil painting from the Dutch Golden Age. The notes that accompanied the image told me it was a 1633 painting by Frans Hals, titled *Portrait of an Elderly Lady,* and was included in the collection of the National Gallery in Washington.

The subject is shown in formal seventeenth-century dress: a black gown, a stiff wire-backed ruff at her neck, a modest white cap covering wispy hair, and her hand clutching a book, suggesting she had some education. Her mouth is closed, but she's smiling gently. You can see there's a twinkle in her eye, a slight sauciness in her gaze, that shows she had a sly wit. She would have been a woman of some means. At first glance I thought she looked about eighty years old, with her wrinkles and her matronly form, all buttoned-up seventeenth-century business, but the notes told me that the woman had been approximately sixty when she sat for the painting. Her real name has been lost to history, but her portrait is believed to have been a companion to a second portrait, most likely that of her husband.

I fell in love with her.

"She's perfect. That's her," I said. "Look at her cute little face. She looks like she has a sense of humor. That's Duchess Goldblatt."

"She's great," Naomi said. "But once you start making connections, people will see who you're friends with and figure out it's you in five minutes. Is it critical that you stay anonymous?"

I considered this. I'd recently borrowed thousands of dollars for a divorce attorney. She liked to cup her hands into a pretend megaphone to help her scream at me louder. ("Wake up and smell the coffee!" she'd shout at me. "Stop being an idiot!") I'd sold my jewelry. I'd taken in a boarder.

Strangers were scrutinizing and questioning my bank account statements, credit card statements, tax returns, receipts, decisions, choices, motives, integrity, and heart. I'd lost my family, my dear ones, my livelihood, and was about to lose my home.

Friends, even friends I'd had since childhood, had turned tail and disappeared. My husband's friends and relations slipped away from me during the split, even the ones I'd thought were genuinely attached to me, but so, too, did many of my own circle: my friends, my dear ones, the people my grandmother would have called my *girlfriends*. Some of my friends hadn't been wild about my choice of husband to begin with, but now they were furious at me for letting my life fall into such a shambles. How could I have been so careless? Men can be careless, not women. Women have to hold the world steady, or the whole operation will spin right off its axis.

("Are you sure you want to do this?" one of them asked me on my wedding day.

"Yes, of course I want to get married," I'd said.

She rolled her eyes and snorted. "You're not getting married, though, right, as much as you're becoming the single mother of a seven-year-old boy." She thought I was signing up for a lifelong burden instead of a partner. I laughed. I repeated that story for years afterwards. I thought she was joking. It's possible, in hindsight, that I've never understood anything.)

I'd had very small hopes for my life. I hoped to be married and I hoped to have a child, just one child — to be an only child was my own lifelong dream; I'd always thought siblings were about the worst thing you could ever do to a kid. Being married meant everything. It meant I would have safely navigated childhood and set down an anchor in a safe harbor: a family, a home, another person who was willingly tethered to me.

I tried to express this in a letter of gratitude and joy I wrote to all the friends who came to a big milestone birthday party for me. So what if I'd thrown the party for myself? I didn't mind. I'd never had one before. I'd thrown a baby shower for myself when I was pregnant, too, when it became clear no one else was going to do it for me. And it's still a party if you throw it for yourself, isn't it? Nobody gets everything they want in life. Lucy never got to be in the nightclub act. Ethel deserved better than Fred. Sure, Lucy and Ethel got fired from the candy factory, but it was a terrible job anyway.

Did we have a happy marriage? I thought so. My ex-husband says we didn't. I guess that difference in perspective tells you all you need to know. I do remember being floored when he told me he wanted a divorce. We had moved into a huge new house only a few weeks before. The boxes weren't even unpacked. All I could say was "Why?" The rug had been pulled out from under me, and beneath that the floorboards, and beneath that the foundation, and the ground, the earth itself, even the 5,000-degree ball of iron and nickel at its core was a little shaky.

The reason he gave me was that I'd spent too much money on a new couch.

"Can't you return the couch?" my mother-in-law said to me on the phone, sobbing.

"I could return it," I said. "But I don't think it's the couch."

"He told us you went ahead and bought a couch he didn't want," she said.

"He was with me. We bought it together."

"Just return the couch. He doesn't like it," she said.

"Okay, I'm hearing you say that," I said. "I'm thinking it's something else besides the couch."

People tried really hard to stay neutral and remain friendly with both of us, but that wasn't going to be allowed. My husband wanted a clean break: nothing to do with me or with anyone who continued to be friendly with me. Everyone had to choose. People started to peel away from this whole sorry mess one by one, two by two. (It can't be about the couch! Who gets divorced over a couch? And they just bought the new house! He was always devoted to her. She must have done something but he's not saying what.)

"You're overhoused," my attorney said. "Sell the house."

"I understand, but we just moved in," I said. "I can't uproot my son again, move him again."

"Sure you can. What did you need such a big house for, anyway?"

"My husband has a huge family," I said. "We thought we'd have big Thanksgiving dinners and Christmas parties, lots of people over all the time. Last Christmas there were seventy people at dinner."

"Look on the bright side. Now you don't have to cook for seventy people," she said.

"My son needs stability," I told her. "All this change is so hard on him. Plus the house needs a ton of work. We were planning to fix it up over time. Who would want it now but a flipper looking for a bargain? Can I hold on to the house for a year?"

She thought about it. "Your husband wants his name off the mortgage. If you can figure out a way to keep it for a year by yourself, and then sell it, okay." She was refilling an elaborate fountain pen from a little pot of ink. Who does that? I thought. She's going to get ink all over her fingers. I couldn't take my eyes off her hands, which might have been the point of that ridiculous pen. She wore rings with diamonds the size of Scrabble tiles.

"I've been doing this for almost forty years," she went on. "I'll tell you one thing right now: Husbands don't leave their wives unless they already have a girlfriend."

"Well, that's not the case here, I can promise you that," I said.

"You think so?"

"I know so."

She tapped her pen against the papers on her desk and slowed her speech down for dramatic effect. "Believe me. Husbands do not leave their wives unless they already have the next one lined up."

"No," I said. "Not this time. Not us."

She groaned. Closed her eyes and rubbed at her temples, showing me my stupidity was the burden she had to carry in life. "This is how women end up in poverty."

> A lot of people go very Martha Graham when dancing
> on their enemies' graves. Me, I like flamenco.
> I want the souls of the dead to feel it.

I had a year: a year of painting and patching and cleaning and landscaping so I could fix up my sprawling midcentury-modern house to sell, giving my son and me a chance to catch our breath before starting over again and he started kindergarten. I thought people would rally around me, but they didn't, and I couldn't understand why.

"I'm in crisis," I remember telling one of my oldest friends. "I need you now."

"I understand you're in crisis," she said, "but I didn't get the first phone call from you when everything went down, and that really hurt my feelings."

"I don't even remember calling anybody," I said. "I was in shock. I was panicking."

"You texted your *neighbor* and told her to call me," she said, fuming. "Do you have any idea how embarrassing that was? You hardly know her. And you and I have been friends for twenty-five years. I stood up at your wedding."

"I'm sorry," I said. "Can't you forgive me? Am I really such a terrible person that I deserve all this?"

She seemed to consider it. "I don't know," she said at last. "Your husband says you are. I think I'm a terrible person. Maybe you are, too."

> If you find yourself feeling embittered,
> roll around in a barrel of kosher salt until crusted,
> and then set yourself in a colander to drain.

Meanwhile, when I discussed social media strategy with Naomi, I was receiving rather more feedback, if you will, from a ragtag crew of unwelcome hecklers and malcontents than any person on God's green earth would hope to receive from a ragtag crew of unwelcome hecklers and malcontents. Did I really need to stay anonymous online?

Naomi saw my face. She nodded.

"I feel you," she said. "Say no more. You don't want any pain-in-the-ass spineless sack of shit seeing what you're putting on social media and getting pissy about it."

She was a good egg, that one. You can see why I had taken to lying down on her desk. "Okay. So we'll keep you anonymous," she said. "We just have to think of how."

"What if the first people I befriend are totally unknown to one another and very far removed from me?" I asked. "Even if you traced it back to the beginning of the network, you wouldn't ever pinpoint me as the center. It'll be more like drawing a spiralizer spinning around me. It'll be as if I'm not even there."

She nodded. "Yeah. Maybe. If you planned it so they truly didn't know each other. If they had no connection to one another, and if they weren't in any obvious way connected to you."

I picked a handful of people who I thought might be game to accept a friend request from anybody to weave a loose network. These were people I knew but nobody I knew well: different cities, different connections, people who were strangers to one another. The two or three real-life buddies with whom I'd hoped to connect had no reason to think it was me. They didn't know who Duchess Goldblatt was, and they wouldn't recognize any of her other connections.

A few days later, lonely and bored, I started to expand her persona. Duchess was eighty-one, I decided, and widowed. It felt accurate enough; I felt like I was eighty-one years old in my bones. (I felt four hundred years old in my heart, but I realized that would be harder to explain and, anyway, I'm not heavily into magic realism.) I thought she ought to be a mother; I decided she had a fifty-seven-year-old daughter named Hacienda. Her first husband had died, but Duchess had plenty of boyfriends, a few ex-husbands, many admirers. She was an author, I decided. A famous, beloved author, perhaps one of the most important voices in American letters. Her books were all bestsellers, including her masterpiece, the family memoir *An Axe to Grind,* and her heartwarming meditation on mothers and daughters, *Not If I Kill You First.*

> I'm thinking of taking a lover. Who's got an
> extra one lying around? Check the cupboards
> and the linen closet and on top of the piano.

Life was grim for me in those days. My future was uncertain — at best an ugly slog — but the more I thought about Duchess Goldblatt, the more I laughed. And what a kick it was that people seemed to want to laugh along with me. I'd never done any humor writing. Never even tried. My husband had been telling me for fifteen years I wasn't funny. ("Do you think I'm funny?" I used to ask him. "No, you're not," he'd say. "You're mean." I always thought he was teasing me, right up until he walked out. And then I thought: Oh, wow. He really didn't think I was funny.)

I sat at my dining room table one day and realized she ought to be *from* somewhere, so I claimed her hometown as Klein, Texas, and chuckled to myself in my empty room. No one I knew would get that reference, and I put it there only for my own enjoyment: a little shout-out to the universe to say hello to Lyle Lovett, singer, songwriter, musician, multiple Grammy Award winner, actor, my longtime favorite of favorites, and Klein's most famous son.

I hadn't initially planned to do anything with Duchess other than lurk around and listen in, but I saw pretty quickly that it was fun to post comments on other people's posts. Duchess could say things I would never say. In real life I was a serious professional with bills to pay and a kid, trying to find a good job in a competitive field; I couldn't go prancing around posting absurdities on social media.

But Duchess could. She talked to everyone. At eighty-one, she considered herself one of the world's great beauties — not just a beauty, but a world-class sexpot and cultural icon — and she flirted with everybody. She had strong opinions; she was confident in her own authority. It was safe to be Duchess. I could be friendly and sociable without running any risk of making friends. I didn't want to make friends. I'd already had a few of those, for all the good it had done me, and I had no interest in signing up for more of the same.

> The only way to be reliably sure the hero gets the girl at the end of the story is to be both the hero and the girl yourself.

I asked a psychologist once how it could be that so many people in my life had treated me badly or deserted me when crisis hit. So many people close to me had been abusive, neglectful, or, as it turned out, had secretly hated me and were eager for the chance to jump ship when everything went sideways. What were the odds?

"The odds were pretty good," she said. "Look at who you're choosing. You went out of your way to find people who would treat you badly. People will always show you who they're going to be. Look at your relationships over the past twenty years. There had to have been red flags that these people weren't going to show up and support you. And yet you gave your life to them. You chose them. You have to ask yourself why."

"I certainly don't think I'm choosing abusive people," I said. "I didn't seek this out. Nobody would. Nobody wants to be treated like this."

"No?"

Psychologists, man. They'll never just tell you the answer

even when they know it. They always make you figure it out for yourself.

"No," I said. "Why would I want that? I'm not stupid. I'm not trying to be unhappy. I would have said I was choosing kind people, people who loved me. Good people."

"Maybe they are. Doesn't matter. Quit worrying about them. Let's look at your choices."

"So you're saying it's me. I'm the common denominator. I'm a magnet for terrible people."

"You know, you're very literal-minded. Imagine for a minute that you are fundamentally a good person trying your best, and so is everybody else."

I made a face that said HA! but I kept my mouth shut.

"Okay, let's start smaller. Let's agree that everyone around you is not evil, and the universe is not working as a setup against you."

"For the sake of argument, I'm willing to hear you out."

"I think any time you're trying to understand what's happening in a person's life, anybody's life, you have to look back at the patterns," she said. "You can think of a moment of crisis as an anomaly because it's going to pass, and that's true in one sense, but sometimes it can also be a magnifying glass that reveals to you what was going on underneath the surface all along. Look at your family of origin. Did you have a loving, supportive mother?"

Impertinent question! (My mother hated me. Still, it seemed unsportsmanlike to bring that up now.) "I don't see what that has to do with anything at this point," I said.

"You don't see any connection between your mother and the people you've chosen to be part of your life?"

"No. None of the people around me now even knew my mother. That was all years ago. Besides, I did have my dad, and he was extraordinary. He adored me. He always tried to make up for anything I was lacking. I figure they canceled each other out."

"The research shows us that's not how families work."

"Maybe the research is incomplete. The researchers didn't know my dad. If it hadn't been for him, I'd be a sociopath now. He was a saint."

"Let's try to be extra careful about our language when we're doing this work. Nobody's a saint," she said.

"Incorrect," I said. "The saints are saints, by definition. Have you ever heard of Saint Drogo? One of my favorites. Patron saint of mute people, the mentally ill, and coffee. If that's not a power triumvirate, then I don't know what is."

"Okay, well, setting the saints aside for the moment: I think any time we're trying to understand what's happening in relationships today, and we want to know the reasons for our choices, we need to look back. Everything goes back to the family of origin."

I sighed and looked out the window.

Oh. Them again.

What's that Faulkner quote? "The past is never dead. It's not even past."

"Next time," she said, "try to find a friend who's emotionally healthy. Try to find someone who's fully functional."

"But if they're emotionally healthy and functioning, why would they need me?"

She studied me closely for a minute. "I'm not sure you understand what a friend is," she said.

"No," I agreed. "I'm not sure I do."

2

Sometimes I tie your words in linen with a little
lavender and mint and use them as a poultice for
my weary old heart.

A FEW PEOPLE IN my circle eventually figured out it
was me behind the account, but they weren't interested in connecting with a fictional character on social media.
They may or may not have thought it was a waste of my time
to write this character, but they certainly considered it a waste
of their time to read it. They told me so, flat out. Repeatedly.

I couldn't blame them. Most of them were in school or had
jobs or kids to worry about, or at least a steady workout routine and a couple of dogs.

And if that had been all there was to it, that would have
been the end. I would have gotten bored and dropped Duchess Goldblatt altogether.

But something unexpected happened.

Other people, strangers to me, started taking an enthusiastic interest in Duchess. I hadn't anticipated that at all. I'd been a professional writer for years, and like many writers I know, I was a white-collar odd-jobber: newspaper reporter, freelance editor, corporate writer, grant writer, speechwriter, proofreader, nonprofit arts organization executive, ghost-writer, you name it. I had a mindset for many years that work begets work, so I never turned down an offer, and besides I wanted to put my husband in a position to pay off all his debt from graduate school. (Teamwork, as it were. Small price to pay for building a life together.) For years, I'd worked two regular jobs, plus I picked up side gigs. As a freelance reporter, my byline even appeared in the paper all the time, and, frankly, my work was pretty good, and I say this to you in all honesty: nobody I knew cared.

I remember once I chased a friend down the street with one of my lengthier feature articles in hand, trying to get him to read it, and I later folded a paper copy of it into a fanciful origami bookmark and slipped it into the book he was reading, where he couldn't help but notice. I'd worked on that piece for months, trying to make something beautiful and true out of thin air, but my friend never got around to reading it. A week later, the papers had all been recycled, and everybody forgot about it. And I understand. That's generally the way it works.

So you can imagine that it was a shock to me when, out of nowhere, strangers started extending friend requests to Duchess and responding to her posts. I had no idea who these people were, but you have to remember that the character of Duchess had been imagined as a famous author, so Duchess figured: if people were reaching out to her on social media, they must be devoted fans of her books.

And so she responded to them as if she were any other famous eighty-one-year-old author responding to her readers: graciously, kindly, sometimes a little bit imperiously, and if they wrote something obnoxious or impertinent or mean, she'd bring them up sharply.

She started to attract more attention. Word of mouth brought her new "friends." I had hardly any friends in real life at that point, but Duchess had plenty. She was always careful to remind people that she was fictional, that she only existed on social media, and, no, she wouldn't be going to see their bands or attend their poetry readings or drop by their holiday parties. I didn't get invited anywhere, nor did I maintain much interest in leaving the house, but Duchess was getting invitations all over the place.

"I'm fictional, but my love is real," she told people, over and over.

It was refreshing, really; it was all the fun of having a wide circle of friends without any of the usual obligations or, on the flip side, any of the traditional expectation that I would ever be able to count on them in any way.

Once you let go of hope, you never have to be disappointed again. I'd finally figured out a way to game the system of being a human alive in this old broken world. If desire is indeed the root of all suffering, then without desire, without hope, without even a self, I reckoned, there would be no more suffering.

> It's a terrible thing to get old. I lost another lifelong friend today. And yet I'm sure I put her here somewhere.

I was in a coffee shop one day with my old friend and boss, Chuck, one of the very few people who had stuck by me when everything fell apart, when another guy we knew, Travis, walked in and waved to us. He called out from across the shop, "Hiya, Chuck," and then added a courtly little bow. "And good morning to you, Duchess."

I shook my head at him in panic, but it was too late. Chuck

had caught it. We'd worked together for years. He'd seen the name floating around on social media, but he hadn't ever put her together with me.

"You?" Chuck said. "You're Duchess Goldblatt?"

"It's a secret," I said. "Don't go running around telling everybody."

He rolled his eyes. "Oh my God. Of course you're Duchess Goldblatt. I should have known."

"Don't tell anyone," I said again. "And as for you," I said to Travis as he pulled up a chair at our table, "don't you go running your mouth, either. I don't even know how you found out."

"I'm sorry. I didn't know it was supposed to be some big secret. How many friends do you have on there now?"

"Almost fifty, I think," I said, which made us all smile. I probably haven't had fifty friends cumulatively in my whole life, and those two clowns knew it.

"Duchess got another friend request this morning from a drag queen in California," I said. "She's big with the drag community, for some reason. I consider it a great compliment."

Travis nodded. "I can see why you'd be flattered. Drag queens have a very high standard for humor."

"I'm pretty sure that a lot of people think Duchess is a gay man," I said.

"Why would anyone think that?"

"I don't know. She keeps telling them she's a woman," I said.

"Well, no offense," Chuck said, leaning toward me and lowering his voice, "but you're a little effeminate."

"I'm a *woman*," I said.

"Oh, right. I always forget that. I don't think of you that way. As a woman-woman, I mean."

"No offense taken, jackass," I said.

"Now that you mention it," said Travis, "it might be that way of talking you have."

"What way? Why? Because I refer to myself as prancing through the world in a vibrant, unending hymn of joy?"

"There it is," he said.

"Can I be friends with you on social media?" Chuck asked.

"I'm not on social media."

"Oh my God, you're ridiculous. Okay, then. *Her.* Can I be friends with *her?*"

"No, I don't think so. You're not great at keeping secrets, frankly, and I don't think she'd like it one bit. She's extremely careful. She went to great lengths to remain anonymous."

"What do you mean *she?* It's *you,*" said Travis.

"It's not me. She's a different person. She lives inside my head, that's all."

Travis leaned in over the table and lowered his voice. "It's not *her.* It's *you.* You're Duchess Goldblatt."

"Well, obviously I know that," I said. "We're not an idiot. She knows she doesn't exist."

"You're a piece of work," Chuck said.

"I can name you fifty people online who think I'm funny," I said.

"No, they think *she's* funny."

"When you saw her profile, did you notice she's from Klein, Texas?" I asked.

"No. Why would Duchess Goldblatt be from Texas? Have you ever even been to Texas?" He paused for a minute, thinking. "Does this have anything to do with Lyle Lovett?"

"It's his birthplace."

"Of course it is. You and Lyle Lovett. Like he's ever going to see your little social media account with fifty friends."

"That's not the point. It's for me. It's my little joke between me and the universe. I'm giving a wink and a nod to the
sun and moon and stars."

Lyle Lovett, as Chuck knew very well, had been my favorite of favorites for a long time, more than twenty years.
One of the many times I'd seen him perform, maybe fifteen years ago, it was at an outdoor concert on a warm summer night. It was the kind of concert venue where you could
bring a blanket and a picnic and spread out on the grass, and
it was the first time I'd seen him appear with his Large Band
and a gospel choir. (I'm going to tell you right now: if you ever
get the chance to see Lyle Lovett and his Large Band under
any circumstances, do not miss, but particularly don't miss a
chance to see them perform with a gospel choir, outside on
a summer night, when you've brought a picnic blanket and a
friendly Riesling.)

I'd seen him perform live before, many times; I knew every
one of his songs, and I don't know why, but that night when he
was onstage outside and I heard his guitar hit the first notes
of "If I Had a Boat," I cried. I couldn't say why at the time,
other than that it seemed like a dear friend had stopped by for
a visit. Not only did I go to his concerts whenever I could, but
they were the only concerts I went to, his was the only music
I paid for; his, the only songs I knew by heart. (We live in an
age of specialization, folks. I've never pretended to be well-
rounded.)

> My birth in Klein was a quick leap from thought to being:
> Athena from the head of Zeus.

In the hospital delivery room, the anesthesiologist stood close
to me, right next to my head, his eyes watching the monitors.

"You can tell a lot about a marriage in the moment when

the husband walks into the delivery room," he said to me quietly.

"Really?"

"Yeah. You'd be surprised how much we see in here."

"What do you mean?"

"Look over here. See, I'm watching your heart rate," he said, pointing at the screen. He spoke so quietly that no one else could hear him. "When he walked in, your heart rate slowed dramatically." He looked back at his monitors. "He calmed your heart."

> I need an app that issues hourly reminders telling me
> which day of the week it is and that sorrow and joy
> are inseparable.

After a while, I got bored being Duchess on that first site. I never got bored with her, per se; I still enjoyed it when people wanted to play along with my nonsense and, remarkably, they did.

But over time, I got worn down by some of the people who latched on to her. Her network stopped expanding after a certain point, which made sense; Duchess couldn't go out and meet new people and add to her circle. The few friends I had in real life with whom I'd hoped to connect via that medium weren't interested, and the conversation became dominated by one or two strangers, stalwarts who (A) were no fun and (B) wouldn't leave Duchess alone. It's a death sentence to any creative effort to have someone looking over your shoulder in real time, offering unwelcome critiques. These people were relentless and without joy, which, as it turns out, is a terrible combination in readers.

The voice of the devil is sweet to hear and he promises you devoted fans, but it turns out they're both assholes.

I don't know what their interest in Duchess Goldblatt was; they certainly didn't seem to take any enjoyment in her. As soon as Duchess posted anything, they'd respond within a minute or two, mostly to complain: they couldn't understand her jokes; they didn't get the references she was making. They couldn't hear her music. Morning, noon, and night, they'd pipe up, over and over, only to log grievances.

"There's the door, sweetheart," Duchess would tell them. "Don't let me keep you. Off you go."

"It's exhausting," I said to Chuck later. "Why would they think I'm interested in their negative energy and their opinions of my writing? Why won't they go away?"

"Because you keep answering them," Chuck said. "Ignore them. You don't even know them."

"I'm not doing it for them. I'm doing it for me," I said. "I like being Duchess Goldblatt."

"Nobody's stopping you from being Duchess. But you don't have to keep responding to strangers online if they're taking the fun out of it for you."

"No, I do have to," I said. "See, that's the thing; I wrote it into her backstory. A big part of her character is an evergreen love for all humanity."

"Okay, Mother Superior. See how far that gets you."

"Plus, she thinks it's important for an artist of her significance and reputation to practice good brand management," I said. "She figures anyone who follows her on social media is one of her fans. She has to talk to everybody."

"You're spending way too much time alone," he said, and immediately cut himself off.

Chuck knew better than anyone how many people I'd lost at that point.

He had been my summer intern years earlier, when he was a fresh-faced college boy, five years younger than me, and I was the only editor at the local newspaper dumb enough to take on an intern. None of the other editors wanted the bother of a student hanging around, but I was sure I could make this kid into something special with a little elbow grease. I went to bat for him and promised the publishers if they hired him for the summer, I'd look after him myself. We've been friends and colleagues ever since. He and his wife used to vacation together with my husband and me back when things were good, or at least when I thought things were good.

Chuck is as loyal a friend as anyone could ask for, which is one of his great strengths. I don't think he's ever let go of anyone. He still travels in some of the social circles I used to be in, with some of the friends I used to have.

I don't think I'm in a circle anymore. I might be in a dotted line now, or just a dot.

> If he's not texting you back, it's only because he's lying, sobbing, in a nest he made from his mother's old bathrobes and cardigans.

I remember being disappointed by the limitations of language when I was pregnant. Everyone talks about feeling the baby "kick." I expected to feel like I was being kicked, which is a hard sensation, the feeling of your foot against my shin, bone against bone. Instead, it felt like someone was moving just past me in a pool of water: someone else was moving, someone else pushing the water nearby. I spoke to him in my mind. I will always love you best, I told him. As long as I live, I'll be on your side. I told him what I looked like: my eyes, my hair, the shape of my face. If you want to, you can look like me, I said silently. No pressure, but you can if you want.

I'd thought for years that I would never be able to have a child; my body didn't seem capable, which I interpreted as a clear sign from God. I figured God must have known what I'd secretly suspected all along: I was fundamentally, irredeemably flawed, and I didn't have it in me to be a mother. I wasn't always sure I believed in God, but I was pretty sure he didn't believe in me, and if God himself didn't believe I could be a good mother, I reasoned, then I had better not push my luck and insist on doing it anyway. Of course, now, so many years later, the position that I had held regarding what I had decided was the will of God appears to me in hindsight to have been, perhaps, a bit extreme. (One of the kindest things anyone has ever said to me was when I was pregnant. "I know you think you can't be a good mother because of your mom," she said. "But I think you're going to be great.")

When my son was born, I was so overwhelmed with joy, I went mute. There's no other way to describe it: I couldn't speak. I didn't speak for hours. We know that in the times of greatest stress, learned behavior will fall away and people move more deeply toward who they really are. I couldn't believe I'd finally been so lucky as to have this child. At last, I thought. At last! My heart is here! My family!

> I've run linear regression analysis and all it produced was the fleeting scent memory of a sudden downpour after a long, hot summer, 1952.

I killed off that iteration of Duchess Goldblatt around Christmastime one year. I sent her over a cliff on a Segway and then deactivated her page on that site.

Sometimes, in the days and weeks after that, I'd think of something perfectly Goldblattian that she'd like to say and miss having the fun of letting her say it, but I didn't miss it enough to go back and run into the same crowd.

I'd done it, I thought. Time to move on. The fun of the game was gone.

But then, maybe a year or so later, my old pal Naomi mentioned a different social media site.

I didn't think much of it at first. I'd heard of it, but I didn't understand how it could work. It didn't seem like there could be much that would interest a serious writer, or any person who cared about sentences. How could you possibly say anything interesting within 140 characters?

"I could see using it for headlines, maybe," I said. "But it wouldn't work for what I'm doing. I have her voice down; I know I can maintain that voice of Duchess Goldblatt. But I don't know how I could sustain a narrative over time when the medium is so ephemeral. One thought at a time, and each one disappears into the ether. How do you maintain a storyline like that?"

"Okay. So don't do it," said Naomi.

"I guess I could look around and see what it's about," I said. "I don't think, logistically, it would work. No one knows the name 'Duchess Goldblatt' on that site. She'd have to start at zero and hope someone starts paying attention."

"Whatever. I'm just saying you could try," she said.

"It seems silly," I said. "Who would start following a fictional character? Even if there were people out there in the world who might like reading her, I can't imagine how they'd find her."

"All right. Don't try," Naomi said.

"Well, it might be fun, come to think of it," I said. "It would be a great writing challenge. It reminds me of a word puzzle. When I was an editor at the newspaper, I used to have to try to edit sentences down, slice out an extraneous word here or there to tighten up a line. Let's say you needed to find two column inches to fit in a new ad that came in at the last minute — you'd have to cut down an article by a word here and a word there to find two inches without sacrificing meaning. It's hard to do it so well that the reader doesn't miss any nuance. But sometimes in cutting for space, I could find a better way to recast a sentence. Working within that constraint, maintaining meaning and nuance in less space, was one of my favorite things."

"Okay," said Naomi.

"I was so good at it, they called me the Widow Killer," I said.

Naomi didn't answer.

"See, in print newspapers, those are called 'widows,' those single leftover words at the end of the sentence that drop down into the next line," I explained.

"Did anybody at the newspaper really call you the Widow Killer?"

"I kept suggesting it, but it never caught on, to be honest," I said. "Let me look into this thing and get back to you."

Naomi nodded. "Right."

> When I edit, I remove the words that don't want to be
> there, hand wash them in warm water, and lay them flat
> to dry. I might use them later.

I brought Duchess Goldblatt back to life online, and I remember thinking, at the time: I hope someone wants to read this, but probably no one will. It will have to be only for my own entertainment, so I'll write whatever makes me laugh.

This was not false modesty on my part. It was the hard-earned modesty of having been a professional writer for many years and knowing that even if I told every single person I knew that I was being Duchess Goldblatt again, most of them would never read it.

My cheerleaders had been few and far between: two or three college professors, a couple of editors, a few dear relatives.

I don't remember Duchess's first words. They weren't anything too special, but I kept at it: a little thought here, a little thought there. I realized pretty quickly that nobody would find Duchess unless she started up conversations by commenting on other people's posts, so I started reading other people and responding to them. That's how readers began to discover Duchess.

I do remember the first person who championed her: Elizabeth McCracken. The novelist, short story writer, and memoirist had been among my favorite writers for years. Duchess read her regularly and sometimes responded to things she wrote. Elizabeth McCracken understood right away that this was an ongoing fictional character whose story was unfolding in real time, and she seemed to enjoy Duchess. I remember which Goldblattian line it was that she sent out again so that everyone who followed her could see it:

> What's that beautiful Japanese word that means both "regretting your lost youth and beauty" and "too hungover to make coffee"?

I was alone in an elevator in a creepy, darkened parking garage in a dying part of town — the kind of place where the old me would have been clocking the location of the emergency bell, threading car keys through fingers in case I needed a weapon, eyes on my surroundings, afraid of a serial killer getting on the elevator and strangling me, but at that moment I remember thinking, Go ahead and kill me already, let's get it over with, I wouldn't half mind. But when I stepped off the elevator and clicked on my phone out of habit, I saw she'd noticed me. In my old broken heart, there flickered the tiniest spark.

Elizabeth McCracken, I learned, is one of those rare and generous artists who looks for the best in other people and holds their work up to the light, as if to say, "Look at this pretty shell I found on the beach, everybody!" Look here, look at this. Read this writer. I think you might like her.

Elizabeth McCracken held Duchess Goldblatt up to the light, and then other people started to pay attention.

3

> You might have to make a cozy home inside your heart
> one day, and when you do, you'll be glad you didn't
> skimp on the butter and cheese.

A T THE PLAYGROUND: my son, four years old, playing in the sandbox with his pal. He's digging in the sand with a plastic shovel and reciting a string of numbers, over and over, an incantation.

His friend asks him why he always repeats those same numbers over and over. "I passcode protected my mom." As if it should be obvious.

"Why?"

"To keep her safe."

> I've been inspecting area farmers' foliage harvest. This
> year's crops are coming in strong. We should have enough
> color to last all winter.

I'll try to tell you what was happening in the other parts of my mind at that point, as well as I can, as well as I remember. I'd had a loss, or a series of losses stacking up one on top of the other, and looking back at the balance sheets, I'm not sure anymore when I began to operate in the red. When my best friend dropped me? Before that. When my husband left? No, way before that. When my dad died? Before. And yet none of that had broken me. It was being separated from my son, the one critical person in my life, and knowing how it was grieving him, that I couldn't bear. When he was four years old, he used to wail and howl for me, and his father, with the best of intentions, thought that my son would get used to the separation faster if he was kept apart from me. On his nights, he wouldn't let us speak on the phone because he didn't want my son to cry. I can remember standing one night in the rain outside their home, my son in his pajamas at his bedroom window looking down at me and crying, and no one would let me in. All I could do was wave up at him. It was a constant back-and-forth: Sundays and Mondays were days with his father; Tuesdays and Wednesdays were with me; Thursdays with Dad; Fridays and Saturdays with me. It was an impossible schedule, and it never got easier.

As the separation went on, I had started to become vaguely aware that my mind wasn't the well-oiled machine it had once been. Certain lights weren't turning on. My brain and I had always been dear friends — I had an ability to see the big picture and the details at the same time; I could size up people and situations in fractions of a second, and draw connections between disparate concepts; work came easily, everything came easily, even after all those losses — but after being separated from my son, I had trouble stringing together two clear thoughts in a row.

One night, I asked someone to come sit with me. I couldn't

bear one more night alone in my house. She agreed on the condition that I didn't object to her watching TV.

"You'll love this show. It's so funny," she said. I didn't care what she wanted to do, as long as I wasn't in my house alone.

I'd heard of it, but I'd never seen it. Nothing the characters were saying made any sense to me. I couldn't follow the story. There were two characters talking, and I remember noticing one had very dark hair. I kept looking at the darkness of his hair, thinking: That's some dark hair. Boy, his hair is dark. But what's he saying? I could hear the words that were coming out of his mouth, I recognized them as English, but somehow I couldn't understand them.

(This didn't alarm me until a few years later, when I finally caught that show again and watched an episode. It was *Modern Family.* I thought: Oh my God. This was that show I couldn't understand. If you've ever seen it, you will perhaps take my meaning: it's not supposed to be completely incomprehensible.)

Most of the time, I think, the effects of my accumulated losses didn't show. Or maybe they did; a lot of people ran away from me as fast as they could, so I guess the cracks in the façade showed in ways I couldn't see. I must have been on autopilot, but my jobs weren't hard or dangerous and I showed up every day. I know I kept going. There are pieces of those days I can pick up now and turn over in my mind, and when I remember them, I try to put them back together.

I remember a psychologist telling me, "You were so traumatized back when I first met you."

That struck me as a strange thing to say, really, because she met me a good two years after I'd lost my marriage, home, job, relations, and friends, and by that time, I was doing much better, so I'm not sure what she was talking about. I wouldn't have said *traumatized.* Lost, maybe, and sad.

Tired. I would have said I was tired.

"How often do you figure the average person thinks about committing suicide?" I asked someone once, offhand, casually, just to try to gauge normalcy.

"Suicide? Never."

"Not never. Can't be never. Never? Really?"

"Maybe once when you're thirteen years old and listening to too many sad love songs," she said. "Why? How often do you think of it?"

(Seven or eight times an hour.) "Not that much." The thought of dying was a fleeting relief — someday this will all end! — but I knew I wouldn't ever bring that on myself. Being separated from my child was excruciating for us both and I was desperate for the pain to end, but I would never have left him here alone. Never, ever.

So I said, "No, never. Not really. I'm just tired."

> Traditional dress for the Solid Goldblatt Dancers:
> a Dutch cap, ruff, and ankle-length black cape over
> gold lamé thong. Very Martha Graham.

I do remember at one point having lunch with my friend Chaya, who brought me a beautifully gift-wrapped book with a detailed inscription.

"Thank you," I said, turning it over and reading the back cover. "*Make Way for Lucia*. E. F. Benson. This looks wonderful. I've never heard of it."

"Oh, yes, yes, you have. This is the one we talked about," she said, tapping the cover. "Remember? You were so interested. When we were together last, I told you all about it. I told you it's one of my favorites. You said you'd love to read it."

I looked at her blankly.

"We talked about this book for probably half an hour. I

told you about the characters, the humor, how much I loved it, how it reminded me of you," she said. She saw my eyes. "You don't remember any of this, do you?"

I shook my head. "I don't even remember seeing you," I said. "Was it recent?"

Chaya stared at me, and then she looked down at the table between us. She put her hand over mine.

So, as I say: there were connections that had been cut. I've been told since, by specialists, that this kind of thing can happen. The human mind is kind. It will create blank spaces for itself. I think of them as little airbags in my mind, cushioning the tender places where the blows and bruises are.

4

Slide a piece of waxed paper between the left side of
your brain and the right side to keep them from squishing
together and confusing you.

I T WAS, I think, the Sunday before Christmas. My son
was three years old, my husband driving. We were taking a little trip to a Christmas tree farm, driving out on ru-
ral roads. Everything outside was gray; the sky gray, the air
somehow gray, nothing blooming or growing so far north
that late in the year. I thought my boy was dozing behind me
in his car seat. I was mentally planning his Christmas present: I'd been staying up late at night, painting the top of a
train table with little scenes: houses and shops, a farm, for-
ests, orchards, roads. There was just one blank corner left
to be painted, and in my mind, I visualized a pond painted
in different shades of blue, edged with cattails and reeds in
browns, yellows, tans. I was thinking about adding in a small

turtle wading into the pond when the tiny voice in the back-seat piped up.

"I see water," he said.

"What?" I looked out the window. There was no water around us.

"I see water with a turtle going in it," he said.

"Oh my God," I said quietly to my husband. "I was just picturing painting in a pond and a turtle on the train table." I turned halfway in my seat. "I see it, too, honey," I said to my boy. "We're seeing the same thing inside our minds."

I told my aunt the story later on the phone, half expecting her to laugh at me, but she didn't.

She wasn't even surprised.

"Yes, my sister had visions like that," she said. "We could never explain it, but she knew things."

Her sister — my other aunt — had passed away maybe fifteen or twenty years earlier. She'd been developmentally disabled but very sociable, very connected to other people emotionally.

"One time when she was living in New York and we were living in Pennsylvania, your uncle fell down the public library steps," my aunt went on. "He was embarrassed so he didn't mention it to anyone. He didn't even tell me. When we called her on the phone that Sunday, she mentioned seeing him fall down. She told him to be careful so he didn't fall down the stairs again."

"How come no one ever told me that?" I asked her.

"I don't know, honey. It's just one of those funny little things you forget about, I guess."

> Remember when you dreamt you were in love and when you woke, you felt the loss? That was me.

"Remember when we were the same person?" I'll ask my son. Now he just smiles at this old chestnut, but when he was little, he'd say, "No! Tell me the story."

"Before you were born, I used to talk to you inside my mind," I'd tell him.

"What did you tell me?" (He'd heard this a hundred times.)

"I used to tell you that I didn't know who you were yet, but I couldn't wait to meet you. And as long as I lived, I'd be on your side. I'd be your friend."

"And you are," he'd say in satisfaction.

"And I told you what I looked like. I told you if you wanted to, you could look like me."

"And I do!" he'd crow.

"Like Athena from the head of Zeus," I always told him. "You sprang forth fully formed from my brain. You're the best idea I ever had."

> People often come to me seeking the true meaning of life, but I find they're usually satisfied with half a sandwich.

Sometimes I know that events will take place before they happen. I know things in my bones. Only once have I ever had an actual vision, a literal vision, in which I saw something appear in front of my eyes. It was a navy blue and white rectangle with block letters, all capitals, spelling out a word: BOLUS. It stopped me cold. "Bolus?" I said out loud to myself, startled. What the heck did it mean? Later that day, driving out on the highway, I found myself in front of an eighteen-wheeler with the logo BOLUS, the same navy and white letters I'd seen in my mind. It was from a trucking company out of Pennsylvania. It was behind me, then suddenly swung in too close on the left, then cut me off and started weaving between lanes. (If this happens to you, friends, follow my example: I put some miles between me and BOLUS, toot sweet, and got the hell off the road.)

More typically, a little idea comes to me that indicates something will happen one way or another, and when these ideas come, they always end up being right. Let's say I'll call to mind someone I haven't seen in a long time and I know he's getting married, or I'll meditate on someone's name and the phone rings with that person's call.

I spotted an old boyfriend once at a funeral, and I asked him later how he'd known the person who had died.

"I guess I'd rather not say," he said.

"Oh, really." I was intrigued. "I had no idea her first husband was an alcoholic."

"Get out of my head," he said.

There was another guy I worked with whose wife's name I kept getting wrong. I wanted to call her Janet. Every time I'd see her, a few times a year at holiday parties and so on, I called her Janet, even though I'd been told repeatedly that her name was Lisa. I could never seem to get her name right. It didn't make sense; the two names didn't even sound alike. Finally, after they'd been correcting me for a few years, I apologized to the woman directly and said, "I am so sorry. I don't know why I have a mental block with your name. I look at you and for some reason I want to call you Janet."

"You don't have to apologize," she said. "It's kind of comforting, to be honest. I know why you're saying it. Janet was my twin sister who died."

(You might think I would have learned to call her Lisa at that point. No. I'd plan in my mind to say *Lisa, Lisa, Lisa,* and still, what came out of my mouth? *Janet.* Eventually, I had the chance to quit that job and dodge the question altogether, which I don't mind telling you came as quite a relief.)

When I was younger, I used to talk myself out of these

moments of intuition as silly and irrational, or weird coinci-
dences. Now that I'm old, I know that my ear is tuned in to
the universe, but maybe I can only hear songs in a minor key.
Most of the time I don't pull off the road before the truck hits.

> I thought you'd been very quiet lately, but then I realized
> I had turned my phone settings to the factory default:
> inevitability of loss.

And Duchess: How did she do it? I'd pick up my phone in one
hand and write Duchess without thinking too much about
it, often while I was consciously trying to focus on solving a
real problem. I didn't plan anything she said, but sometimes
I'd look back at it and think, Boy, that's beautiful, but where
did it come from? Oftentimes I'd wake up at 3 a.m., pull the
phone out from under my pillow, and sleep-write something
Duchess wanted to say. And then my mind could rest and I'd
go back to sleep. In the light of morning, I wouldn't remember
what she'd written until I saw people's responses neatly lining
up. Sometimes I'd see their responses and think, What in the
world are these people talking about? And then I'd scroll back
and see what Duchess had written in my sleep. It was always
something that made sense within her rational dream world.
Sometimes it was beautiful, sometimes funny or inspiring.

> If your brain slips free of its natural casing, you can
> put it in a little easy-care mesh travel pouch.

The damnedest thing was: she was better than me. I don't
mean a better writer (although sometimes, yes, that too), but
she was a better person. Duchess has perfect compassion and
grace. My father was like that; he used to exhort me to have

greater compassion, to find forgiveness, to love people more fully.

"With all the great gifts you've been given in life, can't you find compassion in your heart for people who have been given less?" he used to say to me.

("No," I'd tell him flat out. What a miserable kid. A wee weaselly worm! A poison arrow in my good father's heart! What I wouldn't give to have him back now, for five minutes, to have a chance to try again. I wish I could show him Duchess Goldblatt and say: See, Dad, I was listening. I heard what you tried to tell me.)

I didn't have my father's compassion or his faith, but Duchess did. She was tapping into something else, an energy in the universe that wasn't my energy. Nobody's ever read my aura, but if I had to guess, I'd say it's probably light gray and covered with lint. I'm exhausted most of the time, impatient, distracted, visiting another neighborhood in my head, always with a slow current of sadness underneath. Duchess is white light. She's fully present. She's something else entirely.

> I left a window open overnight and the moonlight slipped away and now the sun's getting in and touching all my stuff.

I had a lot of testing done when I was pregnant, and not just because I was an older first-time mother. After all, my grandmother was forty-three when she gave birth to her first and only child, my father. She'd hoped and prayed for a baby, and when my father was finally born, he was greeted like the messiah, adored every day of his life. In turn, he was fairly old for a new father when I was born. So I figured I was genetically cut out for geriatric parenthood, and it wasn't my age I was worried about.

"We had a ton of testing done through the hospital. Every possible genetic and prenatal test they had available," I told my aunt, offhand. Just making conversation, as one does.

"Why?" she said, her tone sharp.

It was coded language. I heard both what she said and what she really meant, which was: Why would you have so much testing done unless you're considering terminating if they find something wrong with the baby?

"No, no," I said, equally sharp.

Code for: That's not at all what I meant. That is not what I said.

"I just want to know what I might need to prepare for," I said, which was the truth. If the baby was coming home with any kind of special physical limitations, if I was going to need extra help or equipment, or if we'd need to move to living on one floor with a ramp entrance, I wanted to know. I wanted to be prepared.

But I didn't tell her everything. The full truth was that I knew something no one else knew. I couldn't explain it, so I didn't speak it out loud. I recognized it was irrational. The very idea was disloyal to the warm, loving family I'd married into. But the truth was fully formed in my mind, and I could see it written on my bones.

This baby and I are going to be on our own.

5

Look at you people, drunk on hard cider and undressing me with your eyes. A little bit faster, sweets. I'm not a young woman.

*T*HERE'S A ROOM in my house in which I keep my Duchess fan art. People have sent paintings of her, colored pencil drawings of her, love letters to her. (These are all shipped to her, care of what she calls her "Man on the Outside," who's supposedly the one person in the real world who has the ability to ferry packages to her. In truth, her Man on the Outside is not one person but a collection of willing friends out of town who have agreed to receive packages addressed to Duchess Goldblatt. I can usually get about six months' volunteerism out of any one of them before they get wise and decide they're tired of schlepping to the post office in support of my secret life.)

A lawyer in Texas made tiny illustrations of what she imagined Duchess's book covers look like (those are great; I wish

I could show you: her best-selling inspirational memoir, *An Axe to Grind,* is pink lettering on black with an axe; *Feasting on the Carcasses of My Enemies: A Love Story* shows a disembodied heart; and the lovingly rendered family memoir, *Not If I Kill You First,* has a pistol shooting off a daisy), and she whittled a tiny wooden pig for Duchess one day. People have sent candy, postcards, poetry collections, signed copies of books. A woman named PJ in Galveston, Texas, printed out Duchess's picture, laminated it, glued it onto a stick, and carried it around Paris and New York, taking selfies with Duchess everywhere she went. A restaurant called the Ladybird Diner named a pie after Duchess. (Please visit the Ladybird Diner in Lawrence, Kansas, if you ever get a chance. Tell them Duchess Goldblatt sent you.) The novelist Celeste Ng crocheted a tiny Duchess Goldblatt doll and offered to send it to me, but I couldn't accept it; it was part of a set she'd made with a tiny crocheted Princess Leia, and it needed to stay with the group. (I did ask her to make a second one a year later, and she did and then mailed it to the writer Laura Lippman as her Goldblatt Prize. It makes me laugh out loud to know that Laura Lippman has a handmade Duchess Goldblatt doll in her house.)

Crooked Path, by the way, is a fictional town in New York, located both ten minutes north of Manhattan and ten minutes south of the Canadian border, which (if you don't have a map handy) is conveniently impossible. She claims the town was founded by a sect of anti-cartography zealots who were fervently against mapmaking of any kind. Crooked Path somehow shares a border with Kansas and maintains its own navy. It's home to the Crooked Path Home for Aged and Unpleasant Ex-Husbands; the Gertrude Stein Opera Is Opera Is Opera House; the Dorothy Parker Academy for Girls, where Duchess gives an annual Christmas lecture on the sanctity of hiding assets during marriage; and both the Crooked Path

Cat Sanctuary and the (unrelated) Crooked Path Actuary Sanctuary, where actuaries live out their days in peace, prancing through fields and calculating risk. The town has a day spa specializing in the therapeutic laying on of obese dachshunds. Crooked Path also hosts an annual Vodka Festival, a Riesling Festival, and a very popular Living Jenga Pageant in which a few frail elders usually break a hip or two.

> Sometimes at 5 a.m., I greet the day by walking the streets of Crooked Path, performing a light medley of Wagnerian opera. I give and give.

"Daddy says it's a good thing you got married, or I wouldn't be here," said my boy, four years old.

"That's right," I said.

"That doesn't make any sense: 'I wouldn't be here,'" he said. "Even if I was a piece of dust or a cloud, I would still be here. I'd still be with you."

"He meant as a human person, as the boy you are now, you wouldn't be here," I said. "But I see what you're saying. You're thinking of yourself not as a body but as a soul. I think you're right."

"I know I'm right. If I look inside myself, I can see my soul," he said. "It's a never-ending spark."

"Yes. That spark is the deepest part of you," I told him. "Your grandpa once told me he could quiet his mind and get to a very deep awareness of himself, separate from his body. I used to be able to do it, too. I could stare and stare at a bright color until I got to this state of being very aware of myself. It felt like deep joy. I don't know how else to explain it. I haven't done that since I was a kid. I wonder if I still could. You should try. See if you can do it."

He was quiet for a minute, looked out the window. "My

soul and your soul can talk to each other," he said. "As long as we tell the truth of our hearts, even when you're in heaven, we'll talk."

"Yep," I said. "We always have. We're always together in our hearts."

> Hopes and dreams need air. Cracking a window in the car an inch and leaving them behind while you run errands will not work. They could die.

The attorney laid it all out for me: what our new life would look like. My four-year-old and I had no choice. Choices are luxuries for other people. Going forward, we wouldn't even see each other every day.

"This is insane," I told the attorney. "This can't be right."

"I don't know what you want me to tell you."

"There are extenuating circumstances."

"Doesn't matter. Special circumstances are only special to you. Makes no difference to the State of New York."

"It's inhuman to take a child this small from his mother," I said.

"*Taking?* What taking? It's joint custody."

"We're mammals. It's a perversion of the natural order to remove the young from their mothers too early."

"That isn't a legal argument I can make," she said. "I told you. I told you husbands only leave if they already have a girl-friend set up. I've seen it play out a thousand times. And you can't control other people's choices."

"I'm his mother and I can't protect him. How is this right?"

"No kidding. I get it. You can't control who the boy lives with half the time. But who knows? Maybe it'll be fine."

"It will not be fine," I said.

"In another year, your son will be in kindergarten. And anyway, there's research that shows the younger the child is, the better off. It would be worse if he was eight or nine. He's too young to know the difference. He won't even remember this."

"You don't know him. You don't understand the psychic pain of being pulled apart from me. He's an old soul. He remembers everything. He knows who his family is. And when the judge hears —"

"The judge won't care. Makes no difference. You know how many kids she sees every day worse off than yours?"

"My son and I are extraordinarily close," I said. "We have a special connection. We can't be separated like that. For days at a time? For overnights? He's too little for this. He's four years old!"

"So what? You want me to walk into court and tell the judge, 'This boy is extraordinarily close to his mother'?" she said with a sneer.

"It's the truth," I said.

"Nobody gives a shit."

"He's four," I said again. "He's extremely sensitive. We're connected. He needs me. This will break him."

"Kids are resilient," she said. "You'd be amazed what children can survive when they have to."

"No. Not for him," I said. "It wasn't supposed to be like this for him. I wanted a family for him. This wasn't the life I wanted for him. He was supposed to have a family."

"You're not dead, all right? You're his family. You do still have him. Just not every day. That's still family."

"It's not enough," I said. "I won't be able to fix this. I can't bear it. I didn't bring him into this world to have him taken from me."

"Jesus Christ," she said, checking her watch. "I don't know what to tell you. It's the best you're going to get."

> What kind of feelings taste best raw? I like regrets on the half shell. Serve them on a bed of crushed ice with lemon wedges and Tabasco.

In Duchess's story, I'd originally placed her in Texas, since I'd wanted her birthplace to be Klein, and I didn't think it would be that hard to keep track of it. But I kept forgetting it's a different time zone, and different weather, and — honest mistake — I was alarmed one day to realize I'd never actually been to Texas. I genuinely thought I had been. I clearly remember visiting a friend from high school once when he was in graduate school, and I thought for sure it had been when he attended the University of Texas at Austin. A few years into Duchess's life, I realized my friend had also earned a master's degree at the University of Virginia, and that's where I had visited him. Texas, Virginia: you know, they're both warm, and far away, and when you have friends who insist on running around to all these different states, it's hard for a person to keep track.

And so one day I got tired of it and decided to move her to New York, where I've always lived. She claimed she'd sold her Texas estate to a group of monks who were software developers. They wrote an autocorrect app that would overwrite anything naughty Duchess tried to write with a Zen koan, as in:

> So I told him to put on the Dick Cheney mask, and show me your face before your mother and father were born.

Anyway, I moved Duchess to New York, to a fictional town, which I knew would be easier for me to maintain. All it needed was a name.

I was sitting alone looking out my window one night at the street below. It was dark out; nobody was around. My street's name was not in English, and there's no direct English translation for it, but I had looked it up once and there are a few suggested meanings that are said to come close. The third or fourth of these is "crooked path."

Crooked Path is a good name, I thought. It sounds almost plausible for a town name, but it's a little bit off, which is very Goldblattian. I made sure there was no real town in New York by that name so that readers wouldn't get confused. I could play around with its geography and time zone and institutions and traditions. Crooked Path, unlike any other place in this old broken world, I could make as beautiful as I needed it to be, and it was mine, mine, mine, all mine.

> It's Nemesis Reunion Weekend in Crooked Path. Some of them haven't seen their archenemies in years. Tonight we'll do a potluck supper.

It was in those years, around that time, that I moved into a new home. You might have euphemistically called it a fixer-upper, if you were a realtor trying hard to make a sale quick before hopping the last train out of town. I bought it almost sight unseen — it was a safe neighborhood, it was cheap, it was not yet on the market but would be soon — I took half a look and offered the sellers their asking price before it was ever listed. My child and I had lost our home; we needed a home; here was a home. The market was tight and there was hardly any inventory available; in the tiny window of time I had, I was grateful to get anything. Once I'd closed on it and walked through the whole house, I realized how filthy, dark, and dreary it was. All the windows had been painted shut. The backyard was filled with garbage and rusted metal: umbrellas and cans, an old children's wagon. The first day, I took down the old kitchen valance curtains and found them full of mouse droppings. I ran out of the house and sat outside on the curb, thinking: I can't do it. I can't start over from nothing by myself again.

"I can't bear it," I was thinking. I meant to say it in my head, but I said it out loud to the empty street. "I can't bear it."

A voice came back to me on the street; I'd call it a voice, but there was no noise. It was more like an idea generated externally that made itself manifest to me. It was that confidence, that grace, that I've since come to know so well; it was Wallace Stevens's idea of poetry, what he called "sounds passing through sudden rightnesses."

The sounds passing through sudden rightnesses were Duchess Goldblatt, and the idea that she brought to me was: "You will bear it. You have to. You will."

My heart calmed itself down, and I thought: Yes. Okay. I have to. I will.

> I am sunlight. I walk in beauty.
> Where there is Duchess Goldblatt, there are no shadows,
> nor any darkness, nor sorrow anymore.

My old neighborhood had been very formal: large houses, big yards. People would drive into their attached garages and disappear within; you'd never see anyone out walking, coming or going.

My new neighborhood, not so far away and in the same school district, was somehow in a different world: smaller, tighter, louder. People were constantly visible. They puttered. Their children played in the street. I tried not to get too chummy with my new neighbors. When I'd see them out in front of their houses, moms and dads in lawn chairs, chatting (and they were all moms and dads, all paired up, everybody with kids), I'd wave to them and keep moving. I was very careful to always be nice but never too friendly. It's better not to get attached. You get too friendly with neighbors like this, and then you've got a problem on your hands when they inevitably drop you. Suddenly you're persona non grata on your own busy street. I didn't dare risk that. Better to be a neutral positive, as it were.

One of my new neighbors, a young mother of toddlers, flagged me down one day with a wave when I was driving to work.

"Oh, God. I'm so glad to see you're okay," she said, leaning against my open car window, a baby on her hip.

"Why wouldn't I be okay?"

"No reason," she said. "Well, it's just that I thought I heard you screaming a couple of nights ago. Around 3 a.m., I was sure I heard a woman screaming. Was that you?"

"No."

"Isn't that funny — it sounded like it was coming from your house. I woke my husband up and told him to go check on you, but he said it was probably just coyotes. I guess a coyote sounds like a woman screaming."

"I wasn't screaming," I said. "A few nights ago? You thought I was in trouble a few nights ago? Did you come check on me?"

"Well, no. I didn't know. After a few days I didn't hear about a break-in or anything, so I figured it had probably been nothing. Bob said it must have been coyotes."

"I didn't hear any coyotes," I said.

"Neither did Bob," she said. "He slept right through the whole thing."

She turned back to her house, and I moved on. I didn't say: You know I live alone with a child. If you thought we were in trouble, why wouldn't you call 911? Why wouldn't you come knock on our door the next morning, just to say hello and make sure?

Just when you think you can't expect less, you have to learn again to expect less.

> Minor floods in Crooked Path tonight. Volunteers are redirecting storm flows with burlap bags weighted with unfulfilled expectations.

"Do you still have all your neighbor friends over every week?" My aunt asks me this maybe once a month.

"No," I keep telling her. She's remembering that I used to have an open house every Thursday night for all the moms in my neighborhood. Front door wide open, refrigerator full, come on in and pour yourself something. Nobody had to bring anything or plan ahead. Some came sprinting over in pajamas after they put their kids to bed.

It's been a long time since any of the neighborhood moms have come to visit. I can't remember when they stopped coming. Five years ago? Six? One of them drifted off after she'd had too much wine and let slip some family secrets she later regretted saying out loud. Another one sent me a note that our friendship had run its course after her husband made the mistake of showing he liked me a little too much, albeit like a sister. (Note to self: don't get too buddy-buddy with the husbands.) A third got upset with me when I introduced someone to her as an "orthopedic surgeon," which she later told me was a shockingly elitist point to make and belied a latent and unforgivable class preference.

These were such flimsy excuses that they didn't make any sense to me at the time, but now I understand that the neighborhood moms were looking for a way out. They just wanted to get away from me.

"She was . . . an untouchable. Not from scorn or fear, but from the obscenity of the loss," wrote Bill Clegg in his novel, *Did You Ever Have a Family.*

That sentence shook me deep inside my bones. It burrowed its way in and laid eggs there. In my town, in my circle, in my own life, I had become untouchable. I printed that sentence out and put it on my refrigerator and patted it fondly, like a favorite auntie, whenever I happened to notice it there and reread it.

> For my visit to the Dorothy Parker Academy,
> I'm trying to choose one of the more joyful Christmas
> carols about the divorce discovery process.

Duchess is a friend to all humanity, which is all well and good as far as it goes, but I don't mind telling you privately here that it can be a real drag for me. She loves the world. I try to love the world. I mean, in theory, I want to love the world and all humanity. I can certainly see how it would be a good idea.

My lifelong training as my father's child has been instructive here. How do you love everybody? Surely you can't love *everybody.* Surely some people don't deserve it.

I used to ask my father about this all the time.

"I'm not sure what you mean by 'deserve,'" he'd say. "You love people because they're people, because they're human beings. Not necessarily because you enjoy their company, which is one kind of love, but because you recognize they're inherently worthy. Every person is inherently worthy. I'd argue it's your obligation, regardless of whether you think it's your job to decide if they've earned it."

We used to argue over the biblical parable of the prodigal son. The prodigal son, to my way of thinking, was a terrible jackass. His brother, the dutiful son who stays home and does the laundry and walks the dog and gets dinner started, gets no credit, no party, no reward of any kind; the prodigal son, who wastes the family resources on booze and drugs (I assume; I don't know what kind of drugs they had access to in biblical times, but I imagine there were naughty hallucinogenic roots to chew on and so forth), comes stumbling through the front door hungover and gets a huge feast and party. Where's the justice?

"Why does the father celebrate the bad son?" I'd ask. "It doesn't make any sense. He's got another perfectly good son right there, a much better son. He should celebrate the better son and punish the bad one."

"Good and bad are judgments that are not yours to make and, anyway, 'better' is irrelevant. He's their father," he'd say. "A father will love all his children, always. Can't you see how joyous it would be for him when his wasteful son turns his life around, comes back home? 'What was lost has now been found.' He loves both of his children. He's been hoping and praying for that turnaround."

"Because he has to?"

"Because he's their father," he'd say.

"But it's not fair. That prodigal son's a real jerk," I'd say, as if my ten-year-old insight would blow my father's mind. My father, who had spent two years studying in seminary before marriage, was not new to this material. As always, he spoke to me with kindness and deep respect, as if all my ideas were worthy of consideration.

"You've hit on one of the greatest challenges we've been given, honey, and it's a tough one," he'd say. "We have to love other people regardless of their actions and without any hope of reward. Even our enemies deserve our grace."

"But you can't love your enemies," I said. "It doesn't make sense. If you loved them, they wouldn't be your enemies."

"That's the point, honey."

"Nobody can do that. It's impossible. The best you can do is just put up with them."

"You could be right," he said. "It might be impossible. But I hope you'll decide you want to try."

My father's memory is a blessing and a balm. When Duchess is at her best, he's alive again.

When Duchess is irritable or sharp or sad, when she cuts people off for being annoying, when she's goofy, when she's tired and lying on the living room floor and can't bear one more person needing attention: that's when she's the most like me.

> It doesn't matter where I stand at any given moment, friends. I'm everywhere. The sun never sets on the Goldblatt Empire.

6

Reverse semicolons seem like a good idea, but as soon as you die, they revert to plain commas and your estate pays 2 points over the vig.

*I*T SEEMED, FOR a number of years there, that in every direction I turned, doors closed in my face. People didn't want me around, and I understood why, sort of. The more I kept losing, the more I kept losing, and nobody wants to catch that disease.

"I'm trying so hard to connect with people," I told my old friend Jackie. Jackie is part of my ex-husband's extended family and she's attached to my son, so I see her now and again if I invite her, and if I make it easy for her, and if she has nothing better to do. She doesn't invite me anywhere, or call me, or, usually, answer my calls. Our friendship is lopsided, and I've pointed that out to her before, and she's agreed with me: Yes. It is.

"I'm trying to make a new life for myself, and it's like this life I'm trying to make doesn't want me," I said. "There's no place that I fit. The world keeps pushing me back out."

"You just have to keep trying," she said. "Make a place for yourself. Find new people to love."

"I don't want new people," I told her. "I want the old ones back."

"That's a problem," she said. "Maybe you can focus on the things you really enjoy doing. What do you enjoy?"

I thought about it. Everything I enjoyed involved other people. There was only one thing I'd ever really loved that I could do by myself, for myself.

"Writing," I said. "I feel like my best version of myself when I'm writing."

"Okay, then," she said. "Maybe that's how you'll find your new place in the world."

> Scientists are very close to developing synthetic jigsaw puzzles, now that those naturally occurring in the earth's crust have been solved.

Slowly, over a period of time — so gradually, in fact, that I didn't notice it happening, and didn't think much of it — a group began to form around Duchess, or perhaps it was many little groups in constellations. People kept using the word "community" to describe it, which I couldn't see for a long time. It wasn't any kind of private club, after all. Everybody was just online on the same site, and conversations were everywhere. I always thought of it as an ongoing cocktail party; you turn one way and talk to this person, and turn another way and talk to that one. (That's the dark side of social media, too; it's both petri dish and loudspeaker for the very worst people in the world.)

So to me, it didn't look like people were gathering around

Duchess; it looked to me like we had all wandered into the same neighborhood bar and were standing elbow to elbow. I was just another person at the party, and by no means the only one using a pseudonym. Most people might not have carried it as far as I did; they'd use their real first name or their location. To my way of thinking, I wasn't doing anything too different than anyone else.

And we all construct identities for ourselves anyway, right? Online and in real life, we decide how to present ourselves, we teach each other how to behave, and we reinforce for one another which ideas we're keeping and which ones we're throwing away. Good manners are a social construct, weekends are a social construct, values and beliefs and democracy, all social constructs, all ideas that we have come to agree to in our various interactions with other humans over time.

Duchess Goldblatt is a social construct, too, as it turns out. I just have to figure out how to bring her with me in real life. She's dying to take the wheel, you know.

> Fictional people can now give blood. Of course,
> we have always given our blood; we have always poured
> out every bit of ourselves for you.

She became a litmus test, if you will; if you liked Duchess's humor, and if you got her jokes and references, you'd probably like the other people who were drawn to her for the same reasons. Duchess's habit of responding to everyone who spoke to her was engendering the feeling of a welcoming, open-door salon in her timeline. It was organic. No one planned it. I certainly didn't plan it, nor could I have, any more than I could plan a successful party for a thousand strangers. It began to feel like a party to which everybody was invited.

So let's say Duchess responds to Person 1 and then to Person 2. Persons 1 and 2 begin to talk to each other. They form a friendship, in view of but separate from Duchess, and it becomes a real-life friendship. I couldn't always see that there were new friendships forming around her in real time because I didn't realize that they hadn't known each other beforehand.

Duchess likes to be at the center of things, so she'd insist that whenever two or more of her followers gathered in real life, they had to call out with one loud voice, "Long live Duchess Goldblatt!"

And they did. They gathered in groups of two, three, four, ten, twelve; at bars and at restaurants and bookstores and museums, they'd post pictures of themselves together. Sometimes they made T-shirts or tote bags with her picture on them, or printed out her picture and propped it up on the table between them. They bought each other's art. They went to each other's book signings and poetry readings and performances.

"My babies!" Duchess would exclaim when they posted their selfies. "My rascals! My loons!" Someone described it to me as being vetted; if you're drawn to join in with the Duchess Goldblatt community, others can make a fair assumption that you have a certain sense of good-hearted humor.

> By the way, the earth got a little crooked and was running an uneven groove in its axis, so I added four hours to last Thursday to correct.

I had a great-uncle by marriage. Let's call him Uncle Joe. When I joined the family, he was old already: crusty and perpetually disappointed and given to scowling and snapping and hollering. He walked stiffly, bowlegged, always with a slight limp after a lifetime of manual labor. The language and expressions and ideas he put forth were those he'd picked up some sixty years earlier, which led him into endless scraps of arguments with younger family members who wanted to remind him how old he was, how out of touch.

I liked Uncle Joe. There was an earnestness about him I found endearing. He saw the world changing around him and he didn't understand it, but he was quick to admit it and ask questions, to try to get to understanding. I couldn't fault him for that. I used to seek him out at big family gatherings and sit next to him.

One time he pulled me aside. One of his grandsons had come out recently, and he wanted to talk about it. Or talk around it, maybe.

"So let me ask you about the, well, I guess you'd call them homosexuals." *Hahmahsexuals.* I was pretty sure he'd never said it out loud before. "Why is it," he said, "they all got to be so arty?" He gazed at me frankly.

"I see what you're getting at, Joe," I said. "I mean, I wouldn't say it that way, but it is true that a lot of gay men are drawn to careers in the arts. I don't exactly know why. I could hazard some guesses, but I've never seen any research."

"But it's true, isn't it?" he said.

"There is some truth to it. Yes."

He slapped his hand down on the table in triumph, and then grabbed my face in both his hands and kissed my cheek. "I knew it," he said. "All right. You're saying it better than I could. I meant the same goddamned thing. Everybody in this family wants to argue with me all the time. You, I can have a conversation with." He sucked his teeth in satisfaction, muttering under his breath. "Finally, someone in this family I can talk to."

We sat there for a minute, and he looked away, then cleared his throat. "You know he volunteers down at the shelter? Serves the homeless dinner. Spends half his Sunday down there. How many young guys today you think are doing that?"

"He's a good kid," I said. "A lot of the homeless people there are mentally ill. Veterans, too, a lot of them."

"That's right. The veterans come back and there's nothing for them. No services. Nobody cares. He's down there helping," he said.

"I know you're proud of him," I said.

"Of course I'm proud of him," he snapped. He looked away. "He's my grandson, isn't he?"

"I always tell him how you brag about him to me," I said. "Whenever I see him, I tell him I know how proud you are of him."

"Do you?" He still wouldn't look at me. "Good. That's good you do that. All right."

When Joe died, I went to his funeral. Well, of course I went to his funeral: he'd been a pal, for one thing, my partner in crime through fifteen years of family Christmases and Thanksgivings and Sunday dinners, football games and weddings and baptisms. But I would have gone anyway. I was still part of the family and assumed I always would be, more or less. I would always be around, after all, would always be my son's mom, my nephews' aunt. The papers had been served, but we weren't divorced, not yet, nor even separated.

When I arrived at the church, half an hour early, the place was already almost full. Joe had been a salty old coot, but he'd been respected in the community and everyone came out to send him off. The six pews nearest the altar had been reserved for family and were already pretty full. I surveyed them from the aisle to see where I might squeeze in, whom I'd sit with, maybe with my sisters-in-law or some of the cousins, and I saw in the third row, alongside all the rest of our family, was my husband with his girlfriend. And between them, my four-year-old son.

In church. In the church of my grandparents, the church my father had loved so well. I don't know if I can describe to you what it meant, what it signaled. It was a deep, searing humiliation, a public erasure, and the full shock, when it hit, was that it wasn't done by one person acting alone.

You always know in a romantic partnership that things could someday go sideways; husbands leave — this isn't unprecedented in the history of the world — but this betrayal was by everybody. My sister-in-law who'd been my friend since our first day of high school. Her husband: I'd fixed them up on a blind date. My mother-in-law, who used to sneak a kiss onto my cheek and whisper in my ear, "You're my daughter." My nephews, whom I'd loved like my own children since they were born. The first cousins, second cousins, great-aunts and -uncles and all the people I thought were my family, too: come to find out they weren't. They weren't ever mine to keep.

Hundreds of people were in church for Joe's funeral that morning. No one from the family acknowledged me.

If Joe had been there to see it, he would have told them all to go to hell, I think. I'm pretty sure.

After the funeral mass, dozens of cars lined up outside to make their way to the cemetery. I waited at the church door for my son to come toddling out so I could scoop him up with hugs and kisses. I think at that moment I still wasn't sure if I ought to head over to my in-laws' house and help serve lunch to the mourners. (None too quick on the uptake there, I know.)

The church was almost empty, the hearse was ready, and finally, finally they came out. Just my husband and son now. My boy ran to me and jumped into my arms for a hug, threw his little arms around my neck and wouldn't let go. My husband started pulling him off me, prying his fingers off my neck, I said, "Give him a minute, it's a hard day, give him a second to say goodbye," but he went on pulling. "Let go. Let go of your mother now. We're leaving. That's enough." I was saying, "Hold on. Relax. Give him just a minute," he was still pulling, my son was still grasping at my neck, and then they were gone.

He walked off with my son in his arms, and now my boy was furious, sobbing, kicking, and screaming for me.

I stood there watching them go. I was afraid if I moved, if I intervened or made a fuss, it would only get uglier and more disturbing. I looked back inside the church and saw that everyone was gone, even the elderly ushers and stragglers. There was no one to turn to, to say, "Did you see that? What do I do?"

Finally, I turned to go back to my car, and there before me in the church parking lot: the dozens of cars in the funeral procession, all lined up to follow the hearse to the cemetery. Every last member of the family had sat there watching, and not one of them opened their mouths.

> I can't talk now. Vandals have gotten into the Crooked Path town square fountain and siphoned off all the wishes.

I got a package in the mail around that time, sent anonymously. No return address. No note. My name and address were typed. It was a paperback book, *Putting Children First: Proven Parenting Strategies for Helping Children Thrive Through Divorce,* by JoAnne Pedro-Carroll. Who would send such a thing anonymously? It had to be someone who knew me, who knew my husband had left, and yet couldn't see me clearly enough to know I was turning myself inside out to put my child first. What kind of person would mail someone a self-help book anonymously? I called around and asked, but no one admitted they'd sent it. It could have been anyone.

Was it possible I'd surrounded myself with monsters my whole life and hadn't noticed?

> The only predictive text I want is that which tells me when and how my enemies will die.

There are opinions I have gathered along the way through experience and observation, like anyone, and then there are fundamental truths that I know on a cellular level. I have had a long history as a carbon-based life form, after all. Birds know when to migrate. A child knows when it's unwanted. In my mind's eye, I can see the piece of paper in my head on which the story is constantly being written. I can see before me the title Duchess gave to her memoir years ago, which she described as a heartwarming meditation on mothers and daughters: *Not If I Kill You First*.

That Duchess Goldblatt, boy. She always knows.

> My overhead is huge. All of Crooked Path is on the take: the bartenders, festival crowds, innocent bystanders. Even the ghosts get per diem.

I went to see a psychic once, for fun, after my dad had died.

"Your father says your mother was very smart," she said, "but you get everything from him." I smiled and paid her the ten bucks for the reading. She had the right idea, more or less, but I knew she wasn't hearing my father's voice. He would never have said something so ungracious. It's true that my mother was smart, but she was also mean, right down to her bones. (Why did your father marry her? you ask. Quite right you are to wonder. I've been considering that question my whole life, and here's what I've come up with so far: it beats the hell out of me.)

There are two schools of thought regarding the night my mother overdosed and ended up in the hospital, having her stomach pumped.

"I took some pills," she said later, "but I guess I didn't do a good enough job."

The first, perhaps more generous school of thought says that she was merely trying to kill herself, but only herself.

Maybe she didn't even know she was pregnant with me.

Maybe she didn't intend to induce an abortion.

The second school of thought — and this is the school of thought to which I subscribe — says that she did.

> Enlightenment is not a state, friends. It's an unincorporated US territory about the size of Guam. I vacation there some afternoons.

7

Turns out if you get an honorary degree, you want to take it as a lump sum. Three honorary credits at a time is a sucker's game.

*O*NE DAY IT occurred to me it would be funny if Duchess Goldblatt established a prize in her own name. Of course she considered it a very prestigious literary prize. She thought it was the equivalent of the Pulitzer Prize or the Booker Prize or the National Book Award. Maybe a little more important than the Booker Prize, now that I think about it; she thinks her taste is better and her brand, frankly, a good deal stronger.

I (or, to be clear, Duchess) mentioned it by private message to her friend Jon, a professor of film studies in New York. Jon — who feels to me like my friend, because he loves Duchess, but actually doesn't know me at all — suggested they might put a real group of judges together to give the prize some credibility.

It would be funnier, I thought, if there are neither real-world judges, nor criteria, nor submissions, and the only credibility derives from Duchess's say-so. She claims there's a group of judges in Crooked Path sequestered for weeks at a time, voting on a secret long list, but, really, I'm just picking books I love. I only give it to American fiction, new or newish, from writers who follow Duchess. Of course, there are other authors whose work I love who don't read Duchess Goldblatt, but I figure they wouldn't get into the spirit of winning a pretend award. Duchess doesn't give the prize to nonfiction — she says nonfiction is only for sociopaths, children, and the criminally insane — that's her having her little sly fun at my expense because I'm a nonfiction writer. I'm the only one who knows she's really making fun of me, and it always makes me laugh to myself, even though I'm, technically, the one doing it.

> One of my drinking buddies is a former Poet Laureate.
> We visit small towns, fill mason jars with children's wishes,
> grant them one by one.

8

> I made a new ice cream sandwich by pressing the memory
> of a first kiss between two ice creams. You have to eat fast;
> the umami is ephemeral.

*T*HE GOLDBLATT PRIZE is an annual award, more or less,
depending on when I get around to it. It was in June the
first year, but the second year I think I was busy at work in
June and it was more like September.

The winners, so far, of the Goldblatt Prize:

Elizabeth McCracken, *Thunderstruck & Other Stories*
Celeste Ng, *Everything I Never Told You*
Alexander Chee, *The Queen of the Night*
Laura Lippman, *Sunburn*

The prize itself is intangible, although I'll stop short of
calling it pretend. I sent Elizabeth McCracken a coffee mug
from a collection designed by the cartoonist Roz Chast,
whom I knew she liked. To Celeste Ng, I sent a pen engraved

with "The Goldblatt Prize." I forgot to send an actual prize to Alexander Chee for about a year, and then I made him a mug with his book cover superimposed with the seal of the Goldblatt Prize.

Meanwhile, her professor friend Jon, you might get a kick out of knowing, has nominated Duchess Goldblatt two years running for an honorary degree at his university. I'm not sure why Duchess hasn't been recognized by academia yet. Probably just an oversight.

> Writers can be a lot of fun at parties, but word to the wise: Keep an eye on your good memories. They'll strip them down for parts.

There's a popular song playing on the radio.

"What's he saying? What does it mean?" asked my son, five years old.

"A pay phone," I said. He was too young to recognize that term, I realized. He'd never seen one. "Before we had cell phones, you'd have to go to a public phone out on the street corner that was there for everyone to share. You'd put a coin in and you could make a phone call."

"No," he says. "'Trying to call home.' What does that mean, 'trying to call home'?"

"He means trying to call the house, the landline. It's a phone that's built in."

"Doesn't make sense, 'call home.'" He kicked at the ground. "Home is a person."

I nodded. That's my boy! "You're right. Home is a person."

> I'm headed up a mountain today to see a famed holy man about some faith healing. I'm not sure what his ailments are, but I'll do what I can.

When I tell you that people were attached to Duchess, that she meant something to them, I'll try to describe it to you the way they've described it to me. They took her into their psychiatrists' offices and discussed her. (Why? What did they say about her? It beats me. I've asked for transcripts of those Duchess Goldblatt–related psychiatry sessions; apparently none exist, which has to be some kind of epic Western medical bullshit.) They printed out her picture and put it up over their desks at work. (I know this because they'd send me photos of their cubicles with her printed picture.) They read her writing aloud each night at their dinner tables. They made mousepads and pins and custom-printed fabric bearing her likeness. They talked about her to their families. Parents read her words aloud to their children at bedtime. They wrote about her in their diaries. Their husbands and wives and mothers and children would ask them, "What's Duchess Goldblatt been up to today?" (I'd say she's been up to a lot by anyone's standards, but I think especially for a person who doesn't exist, she's been productive in the extreme.)

And they wrote her letters. I saved you some.

Duchess —
    As always, you are in my heart and thoughts, and I am sending you such love and light and gratitude for all you have brought me and so many others, and fervently hoping and wishing and my version of praying that you enjoy some portion of that comfort, warmth, and love in return.

Hi, Duchess —
    I've followed you for a while. My friends and I in

DC don't know what to do next. We're an odd group of friends, full of society's fringe elements, even though most of us can pass, so to speak. One is gay, one's a Goth, I'm the nerd, there's a Jewish guy, a black woman, a Lebanese guy, others . . . none of us know what to do. We live in the most powerful city in the world, but it's like a void has opened before us. Thanks for listening, and thanks for being here.

Dear Duchess,

Thank you for reminding me daily of the goodness and great-heartedness of Americans.

Dear Duchess:

I know that you're a busy person, but I wanted to take the time to tell you what you have meant to me. You have certainly brightened my heart. You make even the loneliest feel important. Thank you!

Hello Duchess,

I promise to find the Duchess in the kindness of strangers and to practice random acts of Goldblattian kindness. I have no idea who you are, but I am glad you are here and in our lives. Much love, your grace —

Duchess —

You are the light and the snap this world needs, and I am forever grateful to have found you.

Your Highness,

I was scrolling through your feed, as I sometimes do, looking for comfort. It cheered me up to see the entries in the Duchess Goldblatt Dog Show. And then I scrolled far enough that I came upon your note about being a refuge for the brokenhearted, and so I thought I'd drop you a line. I'm brokenhearted, Duchess. You don't have to reply, but thank you for being a friend.

Sending love —

Oh Duchess,

I have witnessed your generosity of connection and been deeply thankful for it. I wish I had a dog for the dog show. I adore watching your dog and cat events and they will mean more to me now. Duchess Goldblatt has saved me, too, in the most beautiful and graceful way, even now — knowing you and your followers are out there, celebrating kindness and love, and eschewing hate and evil, makes me feel strong and safe and defended (my proximate loved ones are helping, too). Knowing of your perseverance and resilience, and having received your abundant compassion so many times, makes me feel that I can protect the kernel of goodness in me this time around, even if I have to contend outwardly with ugly things beyond my control. Lots of love to you, too, Duchess. I too believe love will win.

xoxo

PS I know you are a busy person with many friends and I have sent this without any idea of reply.

Dear Duchess Goldblatt,

Of course I could not resist emailing you. Fictional or not, you are a beacon of kindness to me and so many others. I don't fully understand how you do it, but you make the world seem safe, gaily witty, and hopeful: i.e. perfect. I am broken-hearted about the eruption of anger and hate in this country. I am worried about all the people I love who might lose access to health-care.

What I want to know is: who takes care of the Duchess, when she takes care of so many others?

Try getting a variance for a metaphorical ledge that can support a narrative with two people who need talking down. The engineers go nuts.

If I reach back across the years, I can extend a hand to my mother when she was younger than I am now, in hindsight clearly desperate, in hindsight clearly unwell, finding herself pregnant again, overwhelmed and exhausted, and I find there's nothing left in my heart but compassion. Visiting that ugly place, uninvited though I was then, I can slide in through the side window today and find peace.

"Homo sum, humani nihil a me alienum puto," wrote the Roman playwright Terence, hundreds of years before the time of Christ. "I am a human being. Nothing human can be alien to me."

Gather all the icicles you can carry and bring them inside. Nurse them back to health in the kitchen sink. Cheer for them when they move on.

"I gave one of Duchess's friends my phone number," I told Chuck.

"Your real phone number? Why?"

"Well, he's an alcoholic," I said. "He's out of work and sort of between homes, and —"

"Jesus," Chuck said.

"He's in a bad way. He needs a friend. I thought if he heard a friendly voice, you know, I could —"

I didn't finish. I don't know what I thought I could do. Talk to him for a while. Help.

"Does he know who you are? Where you live?"

"No," I said. "I see what you're thinking, but he's no threat to me. He's thousands of miles away from here anyway."

He grimaced.

"Relax. Nothing bad is going to happen because I talked to a sad and lonely person on the phone," I said. "You want the truth — I know in my bones I don't have anything to fear from stranger danger. I can see it in my mind's eye. Nothing bad coming to me is going to come from strangers. All my mortal wounds have always been inflicted by the people closest to me."

"You've got to stop taking on people who are projects," Chuck said.

"I know."

"You can't save everybody."

"I know," I said. "But does it cost me anything to be kind?"

"Yeah," he said. "I think it does cost you something. Try taking care of yourself for once."

I didn't answer.

"You know I'll always have your back," he added.

I nodded. I absolutely knew that was true. Chuck was the one who'd thrown me the lifeline of a job when I'd desperately needed one, when I was a wreck, terrified of the future, frantic and exhausted, no good to anybody, both broke and broken.

"And I know you're in there somewhere," he said. "You used to be so quick, so smart. I need you to come back whole. Okay? I need you at a hundred percent. I know you can do it. Promise me you'll take care of yourself. Do whatever you need to do: take time off, whatever. But come back."

"I'm trying," I said.

He kept his eyes on mine.

"I mean yes. I will," I said.

> I paid extra for a phone with regressions instead of
> updates. It prompts me to return to myself as of this
> morning, last week, 1986.

9

You all know me as an evergreen source of light and joy, but Lyle Lovett has begun following Sarah Palin and not me. The wound may not heal.

That's funny.
— Lyle Lovett

Lyle, you have given me great, great joy. There are no words.

AND THEN HE followed me.

So let's say, hypothetically, that your one very favorite famous musical artist, the one you've gone to see over and over in different cities, the one you've followed and cared about and listened to for twenty years or more, suddenly turns around and says hello. I hadn't ever thought to hope that he would notice me on social media; frankly, it had never occurred to me that such a thing would be possible.

Nobody expects the heavens to open up, for the stars in the sky to turn around and make a wish on us.

I'm not ashamed to tell you I cried when he started following me. I called Chuck to tell him.

"That's so exciting!" he said, catching my enthusiasm. "But what does that mean, he's following you?"

"Well, nothing, really," I said. "It means he clicked the 'follow' button so that whatever Duchess writes will show up for him and he'll see it. It means he's aware of me, that's all."

"But he's not aware of you, right?" Chuck said. "He's only aware of Duchess Goldblatt. He doesn't know you at all."

"So? He doesn't need to know it's me. I know it's me. He knows it's someone and he likes her, so therefore we can make a safe assumption that he likes me."

"Oh, no. Don't you dare. She's not you. You always insist she's not you. You always say she's another person who lives inside your head."

"Well, damn it, now she is me," I said. "If Lyle Lovett likes Duchess Goldblatt, then fine: I am willing to admit that Duchess Goldblatt is me."

"Finally! Tell Duchess I'm very happy for you both."

> Please stop shaking your commemorative Duchess Goldblatt snow globes. You know it wakes me up.

Duchess:

Thank you for all your mentions. I love your writing — so clever, so smart. I look forward to your page every day. Keep up your great work. I'll keep following.

Seriously, if you and yours would ever like to come to a show as my guests, just let me know. — Lyle

That would be the honor of a lifetime, my goodness. Thank you so very, very much. One day I will take you up on that! — DG

Please do. Thank you for being so good to us all, Your Grace. I'll sing one for you tonight in Goshen. — Lyle

Now when you say "sing one for me," I feel that I really must know which song it was. — DG

Pardon my slow response, Your Grace. I slept in this morning on the bus after arriving in Madison. It was "If I Had a Boat." — Lyle

!! I would never be able to choose a favorite among your songs, but when I saw you live a few years ago, I heard that one and burst into tears — you know, the joy of meeting up with an old friend at a party. — DG

That's a kind thing to say. I really enjoy writing with you. If you'd ever choose to reveal yourself, I'd be honored to meet you. — Lyle

I don't know why you're so kind to me, but I'm grateful for it. Someday I'll make sure I get to meet you. — DG

Lyle Lovett and Duchess Goldblatt got into a friendly habit of conversing, publicly, online, through comments and shared posts. They responded to one another regularly. Other people noticed the friendship developing in real time and cheered at the fun and absurdity of a musical legend and a fictional character cavorting before our eyes. At one point, sufficiently egged on, I checked Lyle Lovett's tour dates and learned he was scheduled to appear not far from me a week later. When I say "not far" from me, I mean maybe three hundred miles away, which normally would have been too far for me to travel on a whim, but as it happened, the show was scheduled for the first Friday of the month. The state had mandated that my son had to spend first Fridays with his dad, which meant that I would be alone for twenty-four hours. I hated first Fridays at that point more than I hated Sundays. They were lonely for me, but, worse, they threw my son off his schedule, and by Monday morning he was always exhausted from the stress of the extra separation. I knew I'd have no better way to fill the empty hours than to take the day off from work and drive five hours to see Lyle in concert. I purchased a ticket online and messaged him that I was coming.

> Really? I'd be honored to provide tickets and backstage credentials for you and yours. Might we say hello before the show? — Lyle

> You are so sweet, Lyle. I'd die before imposing. I was glad to get a ticket. It's just me. I'll be heartbroken if I don't get to say hello. And here's a secret no one knows. My name is —

> Thank you for telling me. Your secret is safe with me. Let's plan to meet before the show. We can visit after as well, if you like. Let me know when you might arrive so we can look for you. — Lyle

The night before his show, it started to sink in. I would actually see him up close! In person! It was all much too exciting to take in. I remember I was standing in the middle of a group of strangers when Lyle's name came up on my phone with a text message. My hands started to shake.

Are you still planning to be there tomorrow? — Lyle

Well, that's it, I thought. The jig is up. I'm going to die now of a heart attack. My heart will explode into a million pieces, I will drop dead right here in this moment, and I will never make it to meet him. There's no possible way my old broken heart will survive this.

But then I realized he wasn't talking to me. He was talking to her. And she'd never get nervous talking to anybody. She'd speak to him like a peer.

So I let her do the talking.

Of course I'm still going. Are you? I don't want to tell you your business, but I do think the performance will suffer if you don't go. — DG

You're so funny. Yes, I'll be there. I'd hope it would suffer, but the scary thing is it might not. I'm looking forward to meeting you. — Lyle

10

I will die as I lived: laughing at my own jokes and,
if I had to guess, choking on a swizzle stick.

*L*YLE HAD INVITED me to bring someone. Who would I
bring? I had no one. No best friend or sidekick, no partner in crime; no one who'd want to drive hundreds of miles
with me just to meet my favorite of favorites. Chuck's taste
in music ran more toward industrial, the melody of someone banging pots and pans together in an empty munitions
warehouse in Belgium, and, besides, he had young children at
home and a wife who had long since put an end to any spur-of-
the-moment concert jaunts out of state.

And the truth was: I didn't want to share it. The opportunity was absolutely too precious to me to share with anybody. I didn't know anyone who loved his music the way I did.
I went alone.

I wanted to take him a gift, something to show him how

much it meant to me to have a chance to meet him. But what kind of gift?

I surely couldn't think of anything I could buy in a store that he might possibly want. I tried to think of a book he might like. Normally I'd consider a beloved book an appropriate gift for anybody.

But any book that I would choose would be a gift from me, not from her. He was really asking to meet Duchess; Duchess was his friend, not me, and Duchess would never give Lyle Lovett another writer's book. She considered herself America's greatest author. Top five, anyway. She would have gladly given him one of her books, first edition, signed; but, of course, her books didn't really exist.

Duchess thought of herself as a major cultural figure, a star, so I thought about what kind of gift a star might give to a peer. I remembered the classic Hollywood stars. Fans used to be able to write letters to them, care of the big studios, and they'd sometimes send back an autographed 8 × 10 glamour shot. That was perfect. Giving Lyle Lovett an autographed self-portrait would be Goldblattian in the extreme.

I had wallet-size prints of Frans Hals's *Portrait of an Elderly Lady* made, and I signed one with a Sharpie marker:

> For Lyle, xo
> Your friend, Duchess

I looked at it again and laughed. Perfect.

> If you hold an empty wineglass up to your ear,
> you can hear the sound of Duchess Goldblatt laughing.

I reached the city where he was performing and found the venue. It was an old opera house, as I recall, that had been beautifully restored to its full glory. I stood off to the side of the foyer and watched the crowd. The hall was full; couples and groups of friends were standing around. I stood by myself and texted the number he'd given me for his tour manager. I hung out for a while until a man in a suit came out to meet me.

"I have tickets for you," he said, pulling an envelope out of his pocket.

"That's okay. I already bought myself a ticket," I said.

"Oh, no. No, no. You're his invited guest."

"No, I'm happy to support the show and buy my own ticket," I said. "I've been coming to his shows for years. I always buy tickets."

"Absolutely not. He won't have it," he said. He almost seemed nervous. He poked his head into the box office and told them my name, asked them to refund my ticket price, and then I followed him backstage in search of the man himself.

I'd had a dream, a few months before, that I'd met Lyle Lovett in person, and the disappointment on his face at meeting me broke my heart. Of course it never occurred to me that he wouldn't be disappointed at meeting me. He'd have to be disappointed. Duchess is magic, and I'm not. It was tempting to refuse to meet him at all for that reason. Maybe it would be better to let him maintain the illusion he had of Duchess Goldblatt, glorious living fiction.

But, selfishly, I'd loved him for so long, and so dearly, that I couldn't resist the opportunity, although I knew it most likely meant the end of the fun conversations I'd had with him online. I assumed he'd lose interest in Duchess Goldblatt pretty fast. Once he knew the secret, he'd get bored and move on, and I understood that. It was okay with me. Duchess had given me this one extraordinary gift: because of her, I'd get to meet Lyle Lovett for a few seconds, shake his hand, tell him I loved him, and it would be one of the highlights of my life.

It was already more than I had ever thought to hope for.

I followed the tour manager now through the back corridors and hallways of the beautiful old theater, down a set of stairs here and a narrow passageway there. Eventually we got to the bottom of a staircase in the basement, and he held the door for me and then turned and went back the way he'd come.

Standing not five feet away, his back to me, in jeans and a plaid shirt, was Lyle Lovett. He turned around and looked at me.

I burst into tears. Not the elegant weeping of the movies, either; this was no single crystalline tear sliding down an elegantly lit face. These were gasping, weird, ugly sobs, as I stood under long fluorescent tube lights. I gasped and blubbered, my eyes were streaming, my nose started running. I don't know what I tried to say, something like "I'm so excited to meet you" and "Your music has meant so much to me over the years," that sort of thing. Probably the same thing any lifelong fan would say, but it came out as sputtering babble.

He nodded once or twice.

"Thank you very much," he said. His eyes darted past me. He was looking over my shoulder for his manager. I saw that look on his face. I knew that look. I've had that same look on my own face when a seedy character slides down an alleyway toward me after dark. His face told me he was wondering why he'd been left alone with a nutjob on the loose.

He had no idea who I was.

"Lyle," I said, still sobbing, trying to catch my breath. I steadied myself. "It's me."

"Excuse me?"

"It's me." I pointed to myself, stupidly, as if that would help. "I'm Duchess."

His jaw dropped. I've never seen that happen before in real life. His jaw actually dropped.

"You're Duchess?" Lyle said. "I thought Duchess was a little old lady or a gay man!"

That stopped my crying cold. I sighed. "Why does everybody think I'm a gay man, Lyle?"

"I don't know. Maybe because you're so funny. You're so kind to drive all this way to come to the show." He held out his hand to indicate a room across the hall. "Would you like to step in here and visit awhile? Do you have time?"

Did I have time to visit? It turns out, in fact, that I did have time.

The room had couches and tables and large mirrors and baskets of fruit and bottled water; the carpet was brown; there were posters of shows on the walls; I noted every detail of the room, remembered it all so I could tell my future unborn grandchildren someday, if they're good — we'll see about that, I don't know yet; if they're anything like me, they won't deserve to hear the story of the night I met Lyle Lovett, those ungrateful little shits — and we sat down opposite each other to talk. I saw up close that his eyes were a very deep blue, which surprised me.

"I thought your eyes were brown," I said, peering at him, taking it all in. "My gosh, they're such a deep blue. Why did I think they were brown?"

"I don't know," he said. "Did you know who I was before I started following you?"

"Did I know who you were?" I repeated. "I've told you: I love you. Duchess has told you. I'm a real fan. I've loved you for years and years. I've come to see you in concert tons of times. I've always loved you. Your singing, your songwriting, your humor, your grace, everything."

"No, I know you said that, but I thought that was Duchess being Duchess," he said.

"Oh, yeah. I can see that. Duchess does like to talk about her evergreen love for all humanity. But no, when she's talking to you, that's Duchess being me. Or me being Duchess. It's real, anyway. It's me."

"May I ask you some questions?" he said. "I have so many questions."

"You can ask me anything."

"You're such a brilliant writer. I admire what you do so much. Do you know all the people who follow you?"

"Oh, no. I don't know any of them."

"Of course you wouldn't possibly know everyone, but I mean all the people in publishing who follow you. All the authors?"

"No."

"The editors?"

"No."

"What about the critics and the artists?"

"No, no. I only know about six people in the world total. I don't know anybody."

"Duchess is so well connected. I thought for sure you were an author or someone in the publishing world. How did they come to follow you?"

"I have no idea."

"But you know Benjamin Dreyer, from Random House," he said.

"Not personally, I don't know him. Duchess knows him. She's friends with him. I do think it's a real friendship. They seem to have a special connection. But no, he doesn't know my name or anything about me."

"You've never met him?"

"No. I've never met any of them."

"Pippin Parker? Laura Lippman?"

"No. Nobody. I'm telling you. Nobody knows who Duchess is but you."

"I won't tell anyone," he said. "I promise. I mean, you know I told my manager, but he won't tell anyone. And I told April, my fiancée."

I'd figured that already. It's always the case that when you tell a secret to half a couple, you've told them both.

"Okay, but as long as you make sure April knows it's a big secret," I said. "Duchess will kill me if people start finding out. And the secret isn't for my benefit, you understand. Some of the people who follow Duchess really need her to be their imaginary friend. If they find out who it is, the magic will be gone. It will spoil their fun."

"Maybe the magic will be better. They could know you and know Duchess, too."

"Honestly, I wouldn't mind, but they don't want to," I said. "I've asked a few of them I'm friendly with, by private message, if they want to know me, the real me, the person writing this character. And all, to a one, they've said, 'No thanks.' They know it's a real human being writing this character, but they don't want to find that out and spoil it. They want the fun of her remaining a pure living fiction."

"But how do you form these close connections?"

"I don't know how she's doing it."

"You're the one doing it."

"It's not me. I'm not loved like Duchess is loved," I said.

"I'm sure that's not true," he said.

"Okay," I said. (Friends: it is true.)

"What about that other fellow you were talking to the other day, do you know him?"

"Who?"

"A film or television writer of some kind, I think."

"Duchess will talk to anybody. I'm not necessarily even paying attention."

"You told him to snuggle in."

"Oh, okay, I remember saying that. Yeah, I do worry about that guy. I've tried to keep an eye on him. I think he might have a problem with alcohol."

Lyle smiled. "You sound like Duchess. I can hear her voice. And, may I ask, do you have the arc of the story all plotted out?"

"What story?"

"Duchess's story. Where's her story going?"

"I don't know. I haven't planned anything. I just say stuff as it occurs to me. You think I should be planning a story?"

That was a new worry. It hadn't ever occurred to me that I ought to be working ahead.

"You mean you're not writing it in advance?" Lyle said.

"Oh, my gosh, no. Half the time she's just waking me up in the middle of the night because she wants to look at pictures of cats."

"You're writing it off the top of your head?"

"Yeah," I said. "I usually don't even remember it after I've written it."

"She's so consistently good! She's brilliant and funny. But it's the love that people are drawn to. Duchess extends a hand in friendship to everyone. She offers universal acceptance that people are hungry for. It's beautiful, what you're doing," Lyle said.

"Well, I don't know about that. It's fun," I said. "I probably get more out of it than anyone."

"It's more than fun," he said. "You're giving people connection. They're making friendships because of you. It's so important. It's a gift. I'm always delighted when you include me in your conversations. Tell me," he said. "May we continue to correspond?"

"I will die if we don't," I said, although, if I'm being honest with you now: I didn't expect to hear from him again. I figured meeting Lyle Lovett was a once-in-a-lifetime gift, and I was as grateful for it as I could be. I relaxed into the lack of expectations. It was ephemera, a sunset, a shooting star; I could marvel at its beauty and be content to watch it go by. Drop the pearl back into the ocean and it will disappear beneath the water. The universe will reclaim what's not yours. I had become very used to losing people by that point, and I had no intention of getting attached to anybody new. One way or another, everyone leaves. There are hidden benefits to being a fictional person. If people can't find you, they can't break your heart.

> Duchess is very busy today. Nonfictions, architects, and engineers: tell everyone a joke. Fictions: tell the truth for once, for God's sake.

11

Wherever there's organic matter, a water source, and darkness, reality will grow. Get after it with vinegar, baking soda, and dynamite.

I HAD A BROTHER once. He was ten years older than I was, and even in my earliest memories, he seemed to me to be an adult. I will admit to you now, and only to you: I did not love him. I did not hold him in my heart with compassionate kindness. He had demons; for as long as I ever knew him, he was gravely afflicted with debilitating mental illness and alcoholism. At one point during my childhood, he didn't leave the house at all for a number of years. He was clinically depressed, suicidal, filled with rage and grief and a permeating darkness that nothing could lift. His fundamental essence was bent toward self-destruction, and that manifested itself in all his behavior, in every choice he ever made; as much as any person with a functioning mind and spirit can understand that, I guess I did. I've never admitted this to anyone, but I was afraid of him. I spent my childhood with a quiet eye on the local television news programs, checking police sketches, vigilant for a charcoal drawing of a face like his, fully expecting to learn that he was a suspect in a string of violent crimes. When he died, I cried tears that I would have been ashamed to admit were not of mourning but of relief. Thank God, I thought. It's over.

All my life, I'd been secretly afraid that when he eventually, inevitably, killed himself, he'd take other people out with him. I always assumed my name was pretty high on the short list.

> I plan to die by exploding into millions of bits of light
> briefly illuminating my true form: a piece of paper that
> combusts and disappears.

My father loved my brother and was devoted, genuinely devoted, to his care and upkeep, which I struggled to understand. I saw plainly enough that we were stuck with him, but how could we be expected to love him? You could hardly have a conversation with him. Underneath the alcoholic rages and fundamentally skewed view of the world, he was alternately foul-mouthed, sullen, and mean. He had a sharp mind, but he used it as a weapon to bully and belittle people. He was the dominant force in our lives in a million little ways — he set the emotional tone, he decided what we would eat and when, he was the arbiter of taste, he decided who could come to the house — and we danced to his tune to keep him calm. This strategy stayed in place for decades, even though it only ever worked for a few hours at a time. He hated the world and everyone in it, and he hated himself most of all.

(My father's spirit is looking over my shoulder right now and wincing at these words; he is reminding me that my brother never hurt anyone on purpose. My father would have wanted me to mention that to you. I can hear his voice even now: Stick up for your brother. He never hurt anybody but himself. In fairness and in loving memory of my dad, I will offer you his perspective as well as my own: My brother was suffering and he was sick with afflictions not of his creation. He was the saddest person we ever knew, and he was deserving of all possible compassion.)

"Can't you try to be kind to him?" my father would say to me. "With all the great gifts you've been given in life, can't you be compassionate to your brother, who's been given less?"

"You should have given me something I can work with," I'd tell him.

"He's the one you've been given," my father would say.

"I don't want him."

"He took good care of you when you were a baby. You're called to find a way."

I can't, I would think, but would always stop short of saying out loud. He knew I was thinking it.

My father had it worse than I did, in my opinion. He loved my brother with no hope of reward. He found what little there was to admire there — a quick mind, a strong memory — and he rejoiced in it. He knew my brother would never give him grandchildren to enjoy or bring friends around, would offer no contributions or accomplishments of any kind to this world. Dad got nothing from his son that any father might hope for. My brother barely functioned beyond being a malevolent dark shadow hanging around the house, year in, year out.

At one point, my brother was scheduled to be released from involuntary commitment in a locked psychiatric ward. It will tell you all you need to know about the family dynamics that when he announced that he wanted me, his minor-child sister, to go alone to pick him up from the psych ward and drive him to another private hospital, in another city, where a room was waiting for him, everyone agreed immediately.

Nobody would have dared question my brother's judgment, which was considered infallible; he was a dark, brooding alcoholic, institutionalized by the state, but with us he was absolutely in charge. The general consensus in the family was that I ought to be delighted that he'd made a special request for me to pick him up, and I was. I felt flattered.

Other people were available. Maybe one of the adults around, for example. (Not my father, certainly. I knew he was frail. I had been told that he was terminally ill, but somehow I didn't understand that meant he was actively dying.) When my brother asked for me to come and get him from the hospital, nobody stopped to ask: Is this the most appropriate choice for a young girl? Is it in the kid's best interests to send her alone into a secure psychiatric facility to pick up her brother, whom the State of New York has seen fit to commit against his will? (My best interests, I think it's fair to say, were no one's first concern, or second. Or third.)

As expected, I went prancing into the psych ward, somehow pleased and proud of having been chosen for the special honor. I beamed at his psychiatrists and introduced myself with genuine delight. I marveled at the skill with which they had patched him up and made him well again! How proud they must be! I stood aside with one of the doctors and made conversation. Now that it was all over with, I was curious to know what had been wrong with him before they fixed him.

"We've never known what it was," I said. "Is there a name for it? I've never had anyone I could ask."

"I can't discuss my patient with you," she said. "Why don't you talk to him about it?"

"I can't talk to him," I said. "He's out to lunch, dinner, and breakfast. He's an alcoholic. Every word that comes out of his mouth is a lie."

I didn't mean any of that as a criticism, necessarily, but

these were the plain facts of the case. You couldn't get reliable information out of my brother. This psychiatrist had spent time with him. She ought to have known that. And some of my favorite people have been alcoholics, but the disease turns a lot of people into liars. If you're an addict, and you tell the truth about what's happening to you, people will try to get you to stop, and the disease won't allow you to stop. So the afflicted person will often become a chronic liar, and the people around him will become liars, to cover up for him and to keep him comfortable or keep him calm or employed, or keep themselves safe from him, and I was only a kid, but I thought one of the state's most eminent loony doctors ought to know these things.

> Tonight in Crooked Path, we'll all visit our dear ones' graves and lay wreaths made of apostrophes: the symbol of something missing.

I used to stop down at the public library after my high school day ended and read books in the medical section about psychiatric disorders. I was trying to educate myself about what might be an appropriate diagnosis and treatment plan for my brother. I was never able to figure it out, which will not surprise you, perhaps, but it did surprise me. I was a good student taking AP classes, and I had what I'd been told were excellent research skills. The books were all right there in front of me. You'd think I'd have been able to find out what I needed to know.

There was one passage in an old text that has stayed with me. It was about certain types of family dynamics involving young people with mental illness. Mind you, this was decades ago, long before the advent of many of the medications and treatment options we have today. My brother's illness started to manifest in the early 1970s. The world of information was limited to what people could ferret out on their own. Cast your mind back, if you're old enough. This was before talk shows and discussion forums and online resources. The most instruction we could hope for came from essays by a widely published secular humanist named Dear Abby and a few words with the parish priest, who would have had maybe a bachelor's degree in theology or history but certainly no medical training. If you'd never seen crushing psychosis up close, you didn't know what the hell you were dealing with — and, believe me, there was nobody you could ask. Families kept their heads down and quietly did the best they could with what they had.

The library textbook said that it was not uncommon for some parents, acting out of fear and love and confusion, to go to great lengths to keep an impaired young person comfortable and safe from himself. If he developed a delusional fear of stairs, for example, the family would come around to his point of view: they'd decide his concerns were perfectly reasonable, and they'd help him move his bed downstairs into the dining room. That's our family to a T, I thought. Anything to keep him calm. We would have let him burn the whole house down around us if he decided he needed to.

(The question stands: Does the family of origin remain relevant forever? Maybe. I once stood still and watched as a snowball packed with ice flew down the street toward me, closer and closer, until it socked me right in the face. I'd had plenty of time to move out of the way; I saw in advance it was going to hit me. I stood still and let it. The young man who'd playfully thrown it at my head ran up to me and held his scarf up to my bleeding face.

"Why didn't you move out of the way, you goof?" he asked, and I couldn't make him understand: it would never have occurred to me that moving would help. I couldn't stop a snow-ball from hitting me if it was meant to. I will admit to you now that it's possible Faulkner was right. The past isn't over.)

> The final stage of enlightenment for fictional people
> is the full realization of one's own non-existence.
> It means you'll go out of print.

I remember even now what it was like to walk through the halls of the psychiatric ward. I think I might have gone in expecting something coldly sterile like in the film *One Flew Over the Cuckoo's Nest,* which I'd watched by myself; my father had refused to watch it with me.

"When you've seen enough of that kind of thing in real life," he said, "you don't want to see it again in a movie."

The psychiatric ward didn't look anything as cold or inhumane as Nurse Ratched's wing. Getting up there was the most frightening part, somehow, maybe because I was afraid of what I would see; there were locked doors and security guards, and it had a special elevator, separate from the main hospital elevators, with thick vinyl padding on the walls and inside the door. Being in the elevator was like being shut inside a bank vault. But once I reached the ward, I was struck that somebody had tried to make it sort of — what? Non-threatening? Slightly less weird? It didn't feel like a hospital. It felt like a home. An ugly home, sure, or a grandma's basement that a leftover uncle lives in, with mismatched sofas and scratchy upholstery. How overwhelmingly small and human it seemed.

My brother showed me around proudly, showed me his room, the view from his window, the common area with couches and armchairs, the solarium with its drafty windows. He loved living in the psych ward, I realized sadly.

> The moon closes every few weeks for routine maintenance
> and cleaning. What you see then is your memory of
> moonlight, in lieu of what's gone.

Fifteen years later, I went back to the same sprawling hospital
on a Friday night as a newspaper reporter working on a story
about regional hospitals' efforts to improve their security in
the face of biological and chemical attacks, which were getting a lot of attention at the time. The protocols they'd put
into place were impressive, beginning with a separate and self-
contained decontamination unit. The head of the emergency
department ("MD, PhD, MBA," he told me twice) gave me a
tour. He'd suggested that I should visit the ER at night on a
Friday because things were more likely to get "interesting."

When we came to the elevators to the psychiatric ward,
he paused.

"This is my favorite part of the whole hospital," the doc-
tor said, leaning against the elevator doors with his arms outstretched, pretending he was giving them a hug.

"The psychiatric unit?" I asked him. "Why?"

"Because no matter what goes on up there, it is not my
problem," he said, and he laughed at his own joke.

> Structural engineers are a calming presence. They never
> ask if you like their work, or if their oil rigs and hospitals are
> derivative.

After dropping my brother off at the private hospital that day
— and it might have been a private hospital, as I had been
told, or it might have been inpatient rehab, which in hindsight
makes more sense, but the adults around would have just told
me "hospital" because they figured I was too young to know
there was any difference and, in fairness, I was, and I didn't —

I returned to my home city pretty pleased with myself. I think it was a Sunday afternoon, or maybe it only looks like a Sunday afternoon in my memory. (It's hard to tell. Our memories are some shifty sons of bitches.) I'd successfully taken my brother from one institution to another all by myself, I hadn't gotten lost in a strange city, plus I'd gotten all my homework done. A good day's work, as it were.

But before nightfall, my brother had been reported missing by the facility's administrators. They claimed that he'd never arrived. I was shocked for a moment before I realized that it all made sense. He had engineered the whole situation to his liking. That's why he'd wanted me to pick him up alone. That's why he was so cheerful. He knew I wouldn't understand the appropriate measures for taking custody of a psychiatric patient. When we had walked into the new hospital doors that day, no one was at the reception desk to greet us. That shouldn't have been a big deal. All we had to do was wait for someone to come out to meet us. We'd stood in the empty lobby, and in that moment I could feel him panicking, losing his nerve, but he insisted he was fine. It was late, getting dark already, and he told me I ought to leave for the long drive home.

He'd take it from here, he said.

He knew what to do, he said.

He'd sign himself in, he said.

Obviously, I realize now, as an adult, that I should have waited there until someone came to get him. I should have met the hospital staff and introduced myself and made sure they took care of him. I should probably have filled out some kind of admittance paperwork. It's obvious to me now, but at the time, I had never yet signed my name to anything. My father still signed off on my grades. (His rule, not the school's.) I was an undergraduate then, but in a very small way. My father had agreed I could go to college only if it was a Jesuit school where I could be educated by priests and live in an all-girls' dorm. And, besides, none of us had ever successfully argued with my brother. He made up whatever rules he wanted, and we followed along.

He thanked me for the ride. My brother, who had never had a kind word to say to anybody, had thanked me. I'd never heard him say anything nice to anyone or about anyone, and I don't know that I can describe the thrill of it to you now. He told me he was feeling much better, and, in truth, I'd never seen him acting so normal and pleasant. That in itself should have been a gigantic red flag, but I was too stupidly overjoyed to stop and take appropriate note of it. I was so eager to believe all our problems had been solved. I thought: At last! The hospital cured him! Our troubles are over!

What I didn't see: as soon as I turned the car out of the hospital drive and back onto the main road, he took off.

By the time, later that night, that I got to my father, he had dragged himself out of his sickbed and over to the phone so he could call people all over the state, trying to find out where my brother had gone.

"Dad," I said. "I'm sorry. He said he was fine. I thought he was fine."

"You thought he was fine? Honey," my father said. He was straining to breathe.

"He's choosing this. Let him."

He didn't answer.

"He wants to be left alone. Leave him."

"All right. You made your point."

"Stop giving your energy to him, Dad, please. Let him go."

My father lifted his chin, not nodding, but just enough to acknowledge that he'd heard me and he wasn't arguing. He was rationing the little strength he had.

"K," he said.

"Dad."

"He's all alone," my father said.

"So what? He's almost thirty years old."

"Nobody wants to be as sick as he is," he said. "Nobody wants to be so sad."

"Dad," I said, raising my voice. I snapped at him. "Don't you understand he's never going to get well? He is never going to be well. He is never going to get better. Let him die if that's what he wants."

I had never said such ugly words to him, but I was desperate. My dad had gotten so frail. His cardiologist had told me more than a year earlier that he would have been a candidate for a heart transplant if his lungs hadn't been too weak to bear the strain. I knew he couldn't handle the stress of my lunatic brother prancing around the world loose, off whatever new meds he'd been on, doing God knows what to himself, God knows where. My brother had come very close to killing himself the last time he'd tried — if a stranger hadn't stumbled upon him unexpectedly, he would have succeeded — and now he'd been missing for hours. We both knew too well he might be dead already.

I had blown what would end up being our last chance to get him help.

"Sweetness," he said, his voice thin. His eyes welled up. "I know better than you do how sick he is. I know he's never going to get better."

He sounded insulted, as if I shouldn't have forced him through the indignity of saying it out loud.

"Then why do you persist in this?" I asked. "Why can't you save yourself a little bit, for me? Save your strength, Dad. Just let him go. I need you here. I need you to get well."

He looked at me so sadly, and I knew he was disappointed

in me for failing to understand. All the years I'd been his kid, he'd poured his heart into me and he still hadn't been able to make me understand what it means to love somebody without any hope of reward. Even now, today, I'm still trying to learn the lessons my dad tried to teach me.

He lifted his shoulders almost imperceptibly. "He's my son," he said.

> In your dreams tonight, look over your shoulder to the person standing in the shadows. You will know me when the light bends my way.

12

You can make a handsome living as a Duchess Goldblatt impersonator, but it's not an easy life. It's so hard to get the voice right.

*T*HE NIGHT I met Lyle Lovett I was able to stay awhile after the show and visit with him, and it was after midnight when his manager walked me out of the concert hall and down the street to my car.

"I saved you a spot in reserved parking," he said. "You didn't need to park out here on the street."

"Thanks, but this worked out fine."

"Can I recycle that for you?" he said, holding his hand out for the empty Evian bottle I was carrying.

"Oh, no," I said. "Lyle gave me this. I'm keeping it forever."

"You know, he's been talking about you for three days," he said. "He made everybody on the tour read your stuff. All the guys in the band."

I stopped walking. "That can't be true."

"It is. I don't have an account myself, but he showed it to me, and I can see what you're doing, how it's collaborative performance art."

"Collaborative? Performance art?"

"Yes. He showed me the Duchess Goldblatt Warehouse Sale."

I'd almost forgotten. Duchess likes to name things after herself, and she'd claimed she had a "warehouse sale" (offered without explanation; as a fictional person, of course she had no warehouse, nor anything to sell), but her followers got into the spirit and went along with it. They responded by posting pictures of things they claimed to have bought at the sale: all kinds of oddities, weird artwork, collectibles.

"I guess it is collaborative, come to think of it," I said. "I hadn't thought of it that way before, but you're right."

> All proceeds from the Duchess Goldblatt Warehouse Sale support the Crooked Path Cat Sanctuary & the Home for Aged and Unpleasant Ex-Husbands.

I hadn't at all intended Duchess Goldblatt to be a collaborative undertaking, not in any sense of conscious craftsmanship. I cared deeply about her sentences, and tinkered with them until they were as perfect as I could get them, but only to enjoy the satisfaction that comes from doing something well. It was no different than piecing together a quilt just for the fun of making something beautiful out of scraps, or polishing up a stone before skipping it back over the water.

But in truth, I had only been asking people to play along with me to try to fill up my empty hours. Duchess would always find some way to get people to respond to her, usually at times that were hardest for me: the middle of the night, big holidays, Sundays, dates that had special meaning to me. Duchess came to life to save me, and I wasn't writing her for anybody but myself.

> I let my cozy mysteries and haiku have a sleepover, and now the vicar's examining a cherry blossom and nobody's unraveling any dark secrets.

"What is the point of all this suffering?" I asked the psychologist once. "Why am I being punished?"

"The point? There is no point," she said. "You can live to be one hundred and you'll never find a point. And you're not being singled out for some special cosmic punishment, either. You're not that special. Everybody suffers."

"Then what's all this for?"

"*For?* There is no *for.* It just is. I don't think you need to try to assign some deeper reason to it. Suffering is part of life."

"So you're saying it's inescapable."

"No, I think I'm trying to say that escape shouldn't be the primary goal. The goal is that you accept that suffering is part of life and use your suffering to grow in wisdom and depth."

"Okay. Now we're getting somewhere. See, that's the whole thing in a nutshell. I don't want to grow," I explained. "I have literally zero interest in growing. That's why I'm talking to you. I just want to feel better. Can't you just make me feel better?"

"Feeling better is a modern invention, and, frankly, I think overrated," she said. "When people focus intently only on feeling better, they reach for distractions. Overeating, over-medicating, abusing alcohol and drugs, self-harm: all of these self-destructive behaviors are designed to distract. You're not describing the path to enlightenment," she said. "And long term, I don't think it's going to help you feel any better, either."

> The trick is to be superhuman, but only when you have to. The rest of the time I recommend looking out the window. Maybe have a sandwich.

I thought about it on the drive home from Lyle's show: five hours of driving through the quiet countryside. I tend to get tired easily, and I try not to drive in the dark, ever, and certainly not on unfamiliar back roads, but that night I stayed awake until about 2:30, when I finally pulled over to rest my eyes.

I had told Lyle I'd call to let him know I got home safely, but once I got out on the road, I knew I wouldn't do it. What if his phone rang on the tour bus during the night and woke him up? What if the ringing phone disturbed other people around him?

I'd call or text tomorrow, I thought, or better yet email tomorrow. That's it: I'd email him tomorrow. Email is unobtrusive. Email doesn't intrude on anybody's privacy. People can avoid email entirely if they want to.

Lyle called me at 3 a.m. I was curled up on my front seat, asleep at a truck stop, when the phone rang; I saw his name pop up, screamed, and threw the phone on the floor of the car, where I looked at it. What the hell do I do now? I thought. Obviously, answering it was out of the question. Let me be perfectly clear: I love him and he's my favorite of favorites, but even on my best day, even when I'm wide awake, I'm in no way emotionally coherent enough to handle a phone call from Lyle Lovett at 3 a.m.

"It's Lyle. I'm worried about you," he said on my voicemail. "Thank you so much for coming so far to the show. I was so glad to meet you. Let me know you got in okay."

A few hours later, I took a picture of the sunrise from the road: the first rays of pink warming up a gray sky. Lyle Lovett thinks I'm worth being friends with, I thought. Maybe I'm not too tired to go on living, after all.

> Not until people start seeing typos eating out of their garbage cans at night will they regret hunting proofreaders almost to extinction.

When you get married, you start building a civilization. Everyone says you're not just marrying a spouse, you're marrying their family, too. That was the lifelong dream, for me, right there: a family, a civilization. And a child, yes, I hoped for a child, but I also wanted sisters and brothers if I could get them, and cousins, aunts, uncles, the more the better, and a nice mom. I wanted a big, warm, fun, noisy family, with twenty people at the table on Thanksgiving, and family road trips, and inside jokes, and an open house for good luck on New Year's Day, and for a while there, I had it. I wanted there to be a home in this world where I could walk in the front door without knocking. What an unimaginable intimacy it would be to be welcome to walk into someone else's home without knocking.

I had a boyfriend, in my younger years, who came from a lovely family. Maybe you know the type: the always-room-for-one-more, door's-open, help-yourself-to-anything kind of family. His parents invited me to join them for Christmas Eve dinner one year. My mother was furious.

"How dare you enjoy Christmas?" she said. "Your brother can't enjoy Christmas. Who do you think you are?"

It was a valid question. It's perhaps even more valid now. Who do I think I am?

> We have a large community of experimental healers in Crooked Path. They practice the laying on of hands and the whispering of Lydia Davis.

Thank you again for making such an effort to be at the show tonight. I'll email pictures too when I get home. — Lyle

How can you possibly be so fabulous? I met some very nice truckers in the highway rest station around 3 a.m. What a nice sense of camaraderie they had; I couldn't believe it. They were debating the relative merits of crullers vs. fried cakes. Obviously, there's no discussion; a good fried cake is nature's most perfect food, but it was sweet to hear. Thank you for emailing me. I would love pictures. Duchess and I are always on call. Please give my best regards to April. You said she has questions for Duchess. I would love to know what they are. It gives me such a kick, you just can't imagine. It was one of the happiest nights of my life. — DG

I've thought lots about what you said about some of your followers, how they might be isolated and lonely, how they seem to really need Duchess. I've enjoyed reading Duchess even more with that in mind. — Lyle

People are lonelier than I knew. It took me a long time to realize that people think of Duchess as a friend, and that influences my thinking greatly. There are a number of people struggling who are following her, and I am always especially glad when I can tell that Duchess has given them a lift. People tell her privately that they're alcoholics trying to get sober or stay sober, or their marriages are unhappy, or they have a child who's terribly sick. I think talking to Duchess might be like whispering a little prayer into the wind. You know, it's safe. — DG

You certainly give Duchess the quality of being a devoted friend. I can tell she means so much to her followers. I really like your idea of whispering a little prayer. I think you're right on.

I haven't looked at Duchess yet today, but I will now. Please write again whenever you can. A Duchess follower was kind to include me in her response to Duchess's coffee line this morning. I'm always pleased when Duchess's followers mention me on their own. Duchess gives me credibility among the literary crowd! — Lyle

> I'm thinking about auctioning off my handwritten journal of grave misgivings to benefit the Crooked Path Community Orchestra.

"There are some specific things you can do to bring about the most positive long-term outcome possible," my consigliere told me. (Technically, she wasn't a consigliere; she was a child psychologist, but I figured she was as close as I would ever get.) She was coaching me on what to say to the boy about what shared custody would mean and why he wouldn't be seeing his mom every day anymore.

"Well, surely I can always tell the truth. I can't lie," I said. "Lies destroy relationships. You can't be suggesting I should lie."

"The best possible outcome is that he gets through this intact and healthy, and if that happens, it's going to be because you're the one who sees to it. Do you understand? You can say nothing negative to him about other people in his family, and I mean nothing. Never, ever, ever."

"Then what do I say? How do I explain any of this? Adults don't even understand what's going on. I don't understand it."

"When you have to say something, say something kind. Say something helpful. Dig deep."

I threw up my hands and almost snapped, Like what? But something in her eyes stopped me. She held my gaze.

"You have to be superhuman now," she said.

I didn't say anything. She let a minute pass.

"Do you understand what I mean by superhuman?" she asked.

I let my head fall back to lean against the wall. "Yeah," I said. Shit. "I do."

> I remind myself that this has always been a refuge for
> the brokenhearted. If any of you need a friend today,
> let me know.

Of the two hundred white-collar odd jobs I've had over time, one of them involved working with authors. Have I mentioned that? And so over the years I've met a lot of my favorites, and they might remember me, as me, if you told them my name, or they might not. They meet a lot of people, after all. (There are even a few of them who met me in real life, and years later they met Duchess online, but they don't know that she and I are the same person, and I figure they don't need to.) Anyway, many years ago, before I was even married, I got the chance to spend some time with Elmore Leonard, who was not only one of the greats, one of my favorites, but had been my late father's favorite author. In my father's house, the name Elmore Leonard rang out as a folk hero, a cross between a patron saint and a beloved drinking buddy. Whenever a new Elmore Leonard book came out, that was cause for celebration. His books brought a lot of joy into our lives.

Elmore Leonard and I were sitting together backstage at one of his public events, which was a thrill for me, and not because he was famous. It was because my dad had loved him. When someone you love dies, you lose them in pieces over time, but you also get them back in pieces: little fragments of memory come rushing back through what they cared about, what brought them joy. If you're lucky, you get little pieces back for the rest of your life. Some loves you don't recover from. Elmore Leonard and I were just visiting while the crowd out front gathered to take their seats, and he was holding the program brochure. He took a minute to read the description of himself.

"Who writes these programs?" he asked, without looking up.

"I wrote that," I said. I'd done my best, of course, but Elmore Leonard was a writer's writer, as you probably know. He was a brilliant prose stylist and a first-rate mind. I hoped to God I'd managed, in five hundred words, to do him proud.

He nodded, lifted his gaze from the paper to meet my eye. "These are the best I've ever seen," he said.

My eyes filled with tears at that compliment, which I hold dear to my heart even today. Can you imagine what joy it would have brought my dad to hear Elmore Leonard say those words to his kid?

"Dutch," I said — he'd invited me to call him Dutch, his lifelong nickname, and of course I did, even though my father had always referred to the famous author reverently and with love as Elmore Leonard, *my buddy Elmore Leonard,* and it felt a little impertinent now not to use his given name — "Dutch, I know it's a lot to ask, but in all seriousness, would you mind? When you go out onstage, can you say that again to the crowd?"

He chuckled. People always think I'm joking when I'm not.

"I'm serious," I said. "It would mean the world to me. My mother's in the audience tonight, and, honestly, it would just kill her."

He laughed then, a real laugh. I made Elmore Leonard laugh out loud, friends.

Framed and hanging over my desk in my office today is the note he wrote me on that program. I won't tell you what he wrote. That's one gift too precious to share. But whenever Duchess Goldblatt mentions the choir of angels and saints cheering her on, she's counting Elmore Leonard first among them.

> All the lights are dimmed in Crooked Path tonight, friends, and every house a house of mourning. We have said goodbye to one of our dearest.

13

A fun summer activity in Crooked Path is to pack a picnic basket and a bottle of wine and come out to watch me write on a clay surface.

I TOOK A PICTURE of Lyle the night I met him. It's one of my most prized possessions. I asked him to turn and look at me and he did, with a huge, beautiful grin. With his permission, Duchess posted the picture, but she waited a week or so and cropped the image so that no one would be able to identify where exactly they'd met. Instead of admitting she'd attended his public performance, she claimed it had been her event; she said she'd done a public reading and book signing, and Lyle had been one of the many fans who'd come out to see her.

Back at home, I framed his picture and hung it up. I thought it would be perfect to hang it alongside a framed picture of Duchess; they're both honored members of the clan, after all. I printed up one of him and one of her and framed them both, and hung them next to my built-in bookshelves. I didn't think much of it for a week or two, when I passed by and noticed: his picture was a 5 × 7. Hers had to be 11 × 16. She'd made herself more than twice as big as Lyle Lovett.

"You rascal," I said out loud to her portrait, shaking my head. If that wasn't the Goldblattianest move she'd ever made.

> Don't let anyone shame you for your love of an imaginary friend. Religions have been founded on less.

One year, Duchess decided she ought to encourage a gathering of the faithful at the foot of her portrait in the National Gallery in Washington, DC. "DGDC," she called it, and told people they ought to meet up there. Some of them actually did; they gathered at her portrait and took their pictures there, and then had lunch together, I think. One of them wrote to her about it: "I believed that for me there would never again be friends, or love, or trust, or joy. I thought my life was a matter of waiting for it to stop. The Duchess, her joinings, her faith, her words, her friendship, her insistence I not surrender — she has made a miracle and I can never, ever repay her. Thank you, your grace, for all this love and light you have brought to me."

"Why do people call her 'your grace'?" Chuck asked me, reading this over my shoulder.

"They think she's a real duchess," I said.

"They think she's real?"

"Oh, no. They know she's not real. Not real-real. They think she's a fictional character who's supposed to be a duchess. Or they think she's a fictional character who thinks she's a duchess."

"But she's not?"

"No. She knows Duchess is only her first name. I told you I named her after the dog."

"Why don't you correct them?"

"She won't let me," I said. "She loves being called 'her grace.'"

"I think you need more medication," he said.

"Oh, there's no question," I said. "Trouble is they don't make enough."

> Whenever two or more of you are gathered,
> you must raise a glass and cry out with one joyful voice,
> "LONG LIVE DUCHESS GOLDBLATT!"

There's a certain vibe I strive to give Duchess. I saw the singer Anita Baker once onstage, years ago, and a memory of her has stayed with me. It was near the end of her concert, and she'd walked up to the front of the stage where a large crowd of fans was pressing forward with their arms outstretched, all trying to touch her. She held her microphone in her right hand, and while she sang, she leaned over, and with her left hand grasped one person's hand, and then another, and another. One of the people in the crowd grabbed her hand, trying to pull the jeweled ring off her finger. Right in the middle of the song! Anita Baker — unflappable, gracious beyond measure, elegance itself — didn't miss a beat. She said, "No, no, baby," switched the mic to her other hand, and went on singing and reaching out to people.

And because Duchess considered herself a star, and spoke to everyone as if she were one, and insisted she was a famous author and cultural icon — or maybe because a lot of writers followed her and enjoyed the fiction unfolding in real time — people seemed to believe that she was something special. I understand. We all want to believe in something.

They'd offer their best guesses of which famous author might be behind Duchess Goldblatt, which to my mind always seemed suspect. Why would a real famous author pretend to be this character on social media? I'm pretty sure that well-known, established artists don't have time for this kind of nonsense. I don't even have time for this nonsense, frankly, but somehow she sneaks onto my phone when I'm not looking. And the authors that people guessed at were almost always men.

This bothered Duchess because she's vain about her looks and she considers herself a renowned paragon of feminine beauty, as she reminds anyone who will listen.

It bothered me because it wasn't the yarn I was spinning. There must be a contract between us, storyteller and listener: I will do the work of telling the tale as long as you do the work of believing in it. We all must agree to believe that Mr. Darcy is rich, or *Pride and Prejudice* falls apart. We have to agree that Owen Meany is tiny, that Jane Marple is knitting in a small village, that hobbits live in shires, and that Duchess Goldblatt is a gorgeous elderly woman in love with the world and everyone in it.

There have been a few people — not many; I've tried to discourage them as soon as I see them coming around the corner — who seem to think that Duchess Goldblatt is Someone with a capital S: Someone who can help them get something concrete accomplished in the real world. They believe this Someone can introduce them to an agent or help them get published, get their boyfriend to come back, lose weight, quit smoking, find love, be happy.

I can't help them beyond saying kind, soothing things in the voice of Duchess. When they press me in direct messages, I'll remind them I'm not magic, I'm not special; I'll tell them I'm just another person in the world. They email Duchess asking for favors. They ask her to read their manuscripts, their poetry, their short stories; they ask for career advice, they ask her to award them the Goldblatt Prize. Should I take this job, Duchess? Should I move, Duchess? Should I leave my husband, Duchess? My mother is dying, my wife is sick, my heart is broken, Duchess.

How do I save myself, Duchess?

I keep trying to tell them Duchess doesn't exist beyond what can be put on the page, a tidbit at a time. That's all there is or ever can be. It's a grab bag of love and friendship and hope, as much as you can carry away in 140 characters, and it's there for everyone who wants it, but behind the curtain, I'm a regular person standing by myself, and I don't have anything else to give.

> Some of you have been coddled too long. I'm not cutting the crusts off these sentences for you anymore.

I always wish I could introduce Duchess's superfans to my old colleague and friend Bill. He and I worked together for a few years, and from the very beginning, he said he was in awe of my work. He'd read what I wrote and tell me three or four times a day that I was brilliant.

Then he got to know me.

After we'd worked together for a while, he started saying, "Yeah, you're smart, all right. I can't deny it, but boy, only in certain areas, right?"

"I don't know what you mean," I'd say. (I knew what he meant.)

After another six months or so of working together, Bill started sighing at me and rolling his eyes. He'd shake his head and say, "No question that in some ways you're brilliant. But wow, there are definitely gaps. We have to acknowledge there are gaps."

"We don't have to acknowledge any such gaps. I acknowledge no gaps."

"But how do you account for it?" he asked me, his eyes wide. "I mean, has there ever been an actual diagnosis?"

"A diagnosis of what?"

He waved his fingers in a fluttering motion near my head. "Whatever it is you have. Your brain coupled with the rest of it. I mean, I guess you'd call it — what? Would you call yourself an idiot savant?"

"No, I would not call myself an idiot savant," I said to him, my voice as cold as I could make it, but then I had to start laughing. He was a good egg. It's his voice I hear whenever people tell Duchess she's a genius.

Would you call yourself an idiot savant?

14

I try to keep my abiding love for all humanity in one place,
but somehow it always ends up in piles on the dining
room table.

W HEN MY FATHER was dying, he tried to prepare me. He
knew he was dying, but I refused to know it; he tried to
tell me, but I wouldn't hear it. I wasn't having it.

"I want to talk to you about your wedding," he said to me
once.

"What wedding?"

"Someday, I mean. Someday you'll get married. I've been
thinking about walking you down the aisle. I've got it all
planned."

"Okay."

"I think if I have you on one side of me, I can lean on you,
and someone else on the other side, I'll be able to make it."

"That'll be fine."

He nodded. A few days later he brought it up again.

"So about your wedding," he said. "Now that I think about it, I'm not sure if I'll be able to walk. We might have to plan that I'll be in the wheelchair. Someone will push me, and I'll hold your hand."

"Okay," I said. "We'll figure it out. Don't worry about it. It's a long ways off anyway."

And then maybe a week later: "Honey. About your wedding."

"Yep."

He waited until I looked him in the eye. "I'm not going to be there." He had tears in his eyes, which was unbearable to me, so I tried to laugh it off.

"Well, if you're not there, I'm not going," I said. "So you'd better get well and be there. That's all there is to it."

"But I want you to know I'm going to pay for it," he said.

"Stop, Dad. Doesn't matter. There's not going to be any wedding for years and years." I turned to leave the room.

"Sit down. I want to talk to you about a few other things," he started. "When I'm gone —"

"Nope," I said.

"I have to say this. When I'm gone —"

"You're not going, Dad. You can't go. I can't bear it."

"Okay," he said. But he wasn't done. "You're the strong one," he added. "You'll be the one to take care of them when I'm gone. You're the only one who can do it. Promise me?"

I knew exactly what he was asking. He wanted me to do what he had always done: love the people we had been given, and not just my brother, but the rest of the family of origin. Love them with no hope of reward, recognize that they are inherently worthy of love, accept that they're ours whether we like it or not; love them for whatever they are, forgive them for whatever they are not. Keep them alive. Keep them going.

He wanted me to quit school and make it my life's work, as

it had been his, so that he could die with the peace in his heart of knowing they'd be all right. I'd already changed schools once to be closer to home so I could help out. My father was dearer to me than anyone in the world and it was his dying wish, but I couldn't go along with it.

"If I leave school now, I'm afraid I might not ever finish," I said, although what I meant was: I knew if I quit I wouldn't ever finish. I'd been raised to be a servant of the family, as had my grandmothers and great-grandmothers before me. An object in motion stays in motion, and an object at rest stays at rest. If I stopped moving right then, I knew I would stay home, taking care of my brother and the rest of the family, forever, and that would be the end of the line for me.

"You'll have plenty of time for college later on," he said.

"I can't do it, Dad," I said.

"You've always taken such good care of me," he said. "Can't you take care of them?"

I took a breath and looked at my feet. "They'll be the death of me, Dad. They'll kill me if I let them. They will be stones around my neck, and they will pull me under with them."

I was right, and he knew it. And yet we both knew he was right, too; I *was* strong enough. I could have done what he wanted and said yes. I could have carried them all on my back after he died, and I could have made sure they were okay.

But it would have taken everything I had, and I didn't want that to be my life. I wanted to finish school, and not only that, but finish growing up. I wanted a home and a family someday: a regular family with nobody sick and nobody addicted, a real family where everybody wants to be together, in the kind of home where friends could come visit. I knew someday I'd want a child. Maybe someday I'd even write a book. These weren't such big ideas, really, in the scheme of things, but to me they were visions I'd only glimpsed through other people's windows. How do you make yourself a family out of thin air and good intentions? Where do you begin? My brother was greatly afflicted with alcoholism and addiction and debilitating mental illness and I was not; with all the great gifts I had been given, I could not find enough compassion in my heart to carry the one who had been given less.

I was only a teenager, but I saw what was in my father's mind: of us two children, I was, in that moment, the greater disappointment. Nobody expects anything from the prodigal son, but the one who's steadfast has been given greater gifts. We know the dutiful child can do better, and we need her to.

And yet, as he'd always forgiven everyone, he forgave me, too. He nodded.

"Okay," he said. "I understand. You know I had to ask." He squeezed my hand and lifted it to his lips to kiss it. He pressed my hand to his cheek, where I could feel his tears.

"After I'm gone," he said, "if there's ever any way that I can let you know I'm still with you, I will. Look for me and you'll find me."

"I will, Dad," I told him. "I'll find you."

> People often ask me what fictional people see in their dreams. We dream of you.

Last winter, a friend, Bridget, invited me to lunch, which seemed like a good idea at the time. I had recently resolved to schedule one social activity, not related to work, each week, and to force myself to socialize even if I felt like staying home alone. Bridget was an old friend, and if you were raised in an alcoholic home like I was, you might understand that we tend to put an inappropriate premium on longevity in relationships. Someone could be a terrible friend to you, they could do real and lasting damage to you, but if you've considered them a friend for a long time, that could be enough. You're not going to let them go.

I'd told her about Duchess before, but she wasn't in favor.

"I don't get it," Bridget said. "Seems like such a waste of time."

"Part of the appeal of it for me is that I can't read the way I used to anymore," I said. "I don't have the memory for deep reading or reading anything complex. My concentration is shot. But this is fragmented; it's broken up into little pieces and snippets of ideas. It helps, somehow. I can follow it."

"I would never be satisfied with that," Bridget said. "I'd want better for myself. I'd go get another master's degree. Why don't you go back to school? Go to graduate school."

Graduate school? Was she insane? I had a small child. I was broke. My roof had sprung a leak, and the contractor wanted three grand to fix it. I hadn't slept through the night in two years. I had no job security, and the terms of the custody agreement mandated I had to stay in my small town, with its excellent school district, until my son graduated high school: eleven more years. I could hardly sit still with my thoughts for five minutes.

"I'm holding on by my fingernails," I said. "You have to understand I'm barely keeping it together. I've got nothing left over. I don't have anything to work with. Mentally, I mean, I'm exhausted."

"You should be pushing yourself," she said. "Try harder."

"My mind isn't as strong as it was," I said. "I try to read a book for enjoyment, and I can't retain anything, even a simple novel, even if it's one that I've read before. I lose the threads of thoughts. I know what I was like before. I don't have that kind of mental power anymore. My brain doesn't fire up the way it used to. It's like parts of it have gone to sleep."

"Yeah, but meanwhile, you're wasting your time," Bridget said. "You could be doing something that matters. You could be helping people. Go do volunteer work. You could plant some trees, for crying out loud. Do something worthwhile."

"People seem to really enjoy what I'm doing with Duchess," I said, my voice wavering. "They send fan art. They write her letters. They tell me reading her is the bright spot of their day."

"Oh, '*Duchess*,'" she repeated. "It's so stupid. Honestly. I can't believe anyone would read it."

I didn't mention Lyle. I felt unexpectedly protective of him. She was ridiculing something he cared about. Sure, she was criticizing me and my ideas, but that didn't bother me. That's mother's milk to me. I expect it. But Lyle Lovett: no. I could bear no criticism of anything he loves.

"A lot of people tell me what I'm doing has some value," I said. "It's like a mosaic, a kaleidoscope. Little fragments of beauty and fun. It's all I have the attention span for."

She shook her head. "Stupid waste of time."

Look for the patterns. People will show you who they're going to be.

I knew my default setting would be to overlook what she'd said, to give her credit for being kinder to me or more compassionate or more loving than she really was. But maybe longevity in relationships isn't really all it's cracked up to be. Maybe sometimes it's okay to cut people loose.

So I wrote down what she'd said. I forced myself to look back at those notes many times over the months to come, reminding myself. I had to look at it in black-and-white text on the page to see the old patterns repeating themselves: What you're doing has no value. It's a stupid waste of time. Don't believe anyone who encourages you.

What is a friend supposed to look like? Maybe I could still figure it out.

> An ordinary, perfect summer day like today,
> a woman looks around and asks herself:
> Where's my Ethel Mertz?

Duchess:

I'll be around your area this summer. I hope you'll be around then. I've missed seeing you. But I love peeking in on the wonderful family you've assembled through Duchess. April and I have still never told anyone Duchess's identity, except for telling our friend we know who you are without telling her who you are, as you and I agreed last year would be the honest way to handle it.

Duchess is such a unifying force of nature. That's your book, as I'm sure you've already considered: how we can all be connected, how we all are connected by the most basic and most powerful of all, love, and the acceptance that comes with it.

I look forward to the day *you* take credit for the brilliance of Duchess. The whole world will celebrate you.

Xx Lyle

"What are you doing for Thanksgiving?" Chuck asked me that year.

I shook my head once, quick, meaning: nothing.

"You know you can come to our house if you want," he said. "We always have room. The kids have friends coming. People will be in and out all day. Always room for one more."

"Thanks, but I don't think so," I said. "I think I'll just lay low."

My son was with the big extended family on his father's side, which was what I had always wanted for him: the gathering, the noise and fun, the football game, the cousins and aunts and uncles, all the generations together, everyone crowded in. I wanted him to be part of the family party, even if I wasn't invited anymore. I wouldn't let him miss out on it. I'd tried to find a church or a shelter serving a meal where I could make myself useful while he was gone, but the ones in my area only wanted volunteers to help out on Thanksgiving morning, when I'd have my boy home with me. By one o'clock, the soup kitchens would finish serving the day's big meal. The staff and volunteers would be closing the doors and going home to their own families. If I could have pitched in somewhere, that would have been a welcome respite, but in lieu of being useful or wanted, I had no interest in being an extra hanging around at someone else's family table.

It was worse, somehow, to be somewhere I didn't belong on Thanksgiving, with other people not my own, than to stay home by myself and pretend the holiday wasn't happening.

"Well, what's Duchess doing on Thanksgiving?" Chuck asked. "Hosting some big gala dinner party?"

"I don't know. We'll see. Her daughter's in prison, so she doesn't do a holiday dinner."

"Why is her daughter in prison?"

"She never quite says. We know Hacienda is guilty of crimes against humanity, but beyond that Duchess is very cagey about it. She says that as the daughter of a celebrity, Hacienda didn't ask for all this attention and she deserves some privacy. And besides, it was all covered extensively in the media during the course of the trial, so it's part of the public record if people care to look."

"I'm sure." He smiled. "Duchess's daughter's name is *Hacienda?* Of course it is."

"Maybe I'll have Duchess tell people to share pictures of their pie."

"Hey, I haven't had one of your pies in a long time," Chuck said. "You make the best pie. How about making one for me?"

"Yeah, I guess. Maybe," I said, although I knew I wouldn't. I'd lost interest in baking. I no longer had the attention span for it. I'd lose track of how many cups of flour I'd added to a batter, or forget I'd put things in the oven and wander away, letting things blacken and burn. Everything was exhausting, everything too much effort. And there was no point. "Everything hurts," I wanted to tell him now, but I didn't. I knew better. After a certain point, people lose patience with your grief. They just want you to move on.

> Duchess Goldblatt Holiday Hours (please note for your records): at dawn, just before dusk, uncomfortable silences, and Tuesdays, 7–9 a.m.

"It's amazing what people can handle when they have to," Chuck's wife said to me one day. "A neighbor of mine has four different kinds of cancer. Four kinds of cancer! Can you imagine? And she's just as cheerful as she can be. She never complains. It's so inspiring. Everyone loves being around her. Her positive energy is so amazing. Everybody in the neighborhood is pitching in to bring dinner to her family every night."

"Wow," I said.

"I'm saying you should be glad you have your health. That's all that matters."

"Right you are," I said.

"What doesn't kill you makes you stronger. Did you ever hear that?"

"I have no desire to be this strong," I said. "I'd rather let it kill me."

"Don't say that," she said. "That's a terrible thing to say.

The point is, other people have it worse than you. You're not the only one who's lost a lot."

"Agreed," I said.

What else can you say in the face of a neighbor with four kinds of cancer? What do we gain by measuring my grief against yours?

Other people have it worse than you. Chew up your sadness and swallow it. Smile. Bring a dish to pass. What doesn't kill you makes you stronger.

I can hear what you're thinking. How painful was it, scale of 1–10? Why was it so bad? What was so traumatic? I can hear you thinking it because people have been saying the same thing to my face and behind my back for years. *It wasn't that bad, not really. Other people have it way worse.*

Lots of people lose lifelong friends, lose their families, their husbands, their jobs, their money, their homes, their footing, their sense of self, their place in the world. They don't go running around town sprouting extra personalities.

I wouldn't argue with you. I don't know why it was. All I can tell you is that in my heart, in my mind, in my spirit: I broke. I broke into pieces. There are only tiny shards left now, a mosaic almost pretty if the pattern weren't so irregular, in place of what was whole.

Everything hurt except being Duchess. I remember how often I kept thinking, I want to go home, but then I'd remember there was no home anymore. I had a roof overhead but no soft place to land, and no one anywhere who had to let me in. I could retreat only into my own mind for relief. Only Duchess Goldblatt was the salve to my open wounds.

It was in that spirit that Duchess hosted Secular Pie Thursday on Thanksgiving, in which she invited her followers to post photos of their pies. I didn't think much of it in the moment; it was a whim that struck me funny, like everything she does, but as the day went on, it became startlingly touching, at least to me, to be invited in to see a glimpse of people's holiday tables and their pies.

> I do wonder about you, you know: what your homes and friendships look like, what you whisper to yourself when you think I'm not listening.

I sat in my empty house, dark out already at four o'clock, looking at the pictures of people's dinner tables and the pies their husbands or wives or brothers-in-law had made, or those they'd picked up at neighborhood bakeries. People on Duchess's timeline commented on each other's offerings and wished each other a happy day. It was a party that Duchess had thrown together at the last minute, and everyone was invited to her imaginary table in the ether. It wasn't a real party, but it was almost as good, wasn't it? We were together, sort of — in our thoughts, which is all there ever is anyway — and we all belonged there.

The thought that leaps into my mind unbidden is Thanksgiving was my favorite holiday when I was alive, and I have to pause and remind myself that I'm still alive — oh, right; yes, of course I am; I know I'm alive — and I remember again the words John Irving wrote in *A Prayer for Owen Meany:* "Christmas is our time to be aware of what we lack, of who's not home."

> The trick is to be very still, and then the beautiful idea skittering around the edges of my vision will come burrow in my brain for warmth.

Lyle:
Hello, dears. Thanksgiving is a hard holiday around

here. Duchess and I are going to dig deep to try to find something beautiful. Because of our conversations I'm thinking a lot about pie crust and writing and how much they have in common; there are rules you can learn, and then there's the intuition, or muscle memory of what the dough should feel like: your gut telling you when it's right and when to stop touching it or it becomes tortured. John Irving has a book of essays on writing and wrestling — I don't recommend it; it's VERY John Irving, by which I mean if you don't love him already, it's not going to help — but he gets at the same idea of practicing over and over, in writing or in wrestling. Or pie crust, I guess. — DG

Hello again:

We're thankful to know you and Duchess. I know all her followers are thankful for what she does for them and for her just being her. I have read several of John Irving's books, and I agree about his being dark. Isn't the last line in *Garp*, "We are all terminal cases"? I found *The 158-Pound Marriage* really dark. Irving vs. Sedaris is a wrestling match I'd pay to see. — Lyle

> Duchess Goldblatt's Writing Advice: Use all the letters, not just vowels. Spread them around the page until you get the look you want.

"Your mother must be an amazing woman," a colleague said to me one day, out of the blue.

"Why would you say that?" I asked.

"You're so encouraging and nurturing. You're the most encouraging person I've ever worked with," she said. "You make everything fun. And you always assume good will. I wish I'd had a mother like that. My mother was not supportive and nurturing."

"I'm not sure there's a case to be made for causation," I said. "But it's possible you're thinking of my father. He was extraordinary."

When I was young, I knew something was off, but I wasn't sure what it was, so I tried to mimic and repeat what I thought I saw in other people's families. This is a common mistake made by children who grow up amidst mental illness and addiction; they have to guess at how to pass for normal, and that pretense will always fall away sooner or later.

I remember one time a local business owner heard of a scandal that touched my family — a drug arrest of some kind, small potatoes by my lights; I didn't even take much notice of it — and in an effort to be kind, he'd patted my hand.

"Everybody has a black sheep in their family," he said. "Everybody. There's nothing for you to be ashamed of. It's no reflection on you."

I nodded, hiding my smile. I wished I could tell him what I was really thinking: Him? You think I'm embarrassed by him? He's one of the good ones!

But I decided there was some truth to what the man was saying. Addiction and mental illness thrive in darkness. Why should I hide it? So what if my people had problems? I decided I'd go forth telling the truth without embellishment or embarrassment.

The trouble with that strategy was that whenever I told the whole truth, straight-faced, everyone assumed I had to be joking.

I let a college friend come have dinner with my brother and me at one point. I was tired of compartmentalizing, as if I had anything to be ashamed of. Everybody's family has problems, right? I told my friend the truth with full candor. "There's some chronic addiction–related and general-purpose weirdness happening with my brother," I told him, "but there's nothing for you to be scared of. If there's even a hint of any bad behavior at all," I promised, "I'll handle it immediately. At worst it will be awkward, but nothing terrible will happen."

My perception was that the dinner went very well. I was touched, really; my brother hadn't, at that point, had a social interaction with a new person in probably twenty years, but he pulled out his old military-school manners. He was clean, his hair combed. He tried to be pleasant and make conversation, in his own way. I saw that he was making an effort. I considered the meal a huge success.

My friend's perception was different. When we were driving away, I saw that his hands were trembling on the steering wheel. He seemed genuinely rattled.

"What's wrong?" I asked him.

"I'm sorry," he said. His voice cracked and he cleared his throat. "I didn't mean to react so strongly. I've just never seen anything like that."

"Like what? What do you mean?" My heart fell a little. "I told you about him," I said. "I told you he has a lot of problems."

"I know."

"He was trying really hard. He didn't do anything wrong. What did he do?"

"No, no. It's okay. You warned me. I guess I always thought you were exaggerating."

"Oh," I said. "No, I wasn't exaggerating."

"Yeah," he said. "I get it now."

I still wonder what he found so upsetting about it. Honestly, I don't know what tipped him off. It all looked okay to me.

> Are children still taught to diagram sentences? Are
> sentences allowed in schools, or is it all smiley faces and
> snuffling about for treats?

It's no accident, I think, that in fairy tales, the stepmother is
often described as wicked. (We can talk later about how deep
misogyny runs, in our collective imagination, in art and in life
and in the public realm and in the stories we tell our children
at bedtime, but not tonight, sweethearts.) Fairly or unfairly,
when children are small, a stepparent is seen as the dream
breaker. If you intend to step in front of the adored mother of
a young child, in any context, you must take pains to step very,
very carefully. This is what child psychologists refer to in the
literature as not rocket science.

My boy, at four years old, had strong opinions. He had
strong opinions the day he was born and he still has strong
opinions, but he generally keeps them to himself. With me,
though, he shares his every thought.

"It's my job, as your mother, to make sure you grow up into
a good man who has a loving place in his heart for all living
creatures," I used to tell him when he was small. "It doesn't
make me feel good to hear you have hatred in your heart for
anybody."

He'd pour out his reasons, his explanations, his ideas.

"I understand exactly what you're saying," I'd say. "I understand you have strong feelings, and I can see why. You're enti-
tled to have your feelings. Your heart belongs to you. Nobody
else gets to decide who lives inside your heart. You choose
who you want to love."

It's amazing how simple truths resonate with small children. As small as he was, he saw the truth of what I was saying. He'd nod.

"And I know that you love me, and you want to protect

my feelings," I'd tell him. "But it doesn't make me feel loved and protected to hear that you hate anybody. Hating people doesn't help me, and it doesn't help you grow, either. It makes you small and mean. That's not what I want for you. I want you to have a huge, peaceful, loving heart. And the spark of the divine, your soul, that everlasting spark you can see inside yourself? Everybody else has one, too," I'd tell him. "Every human person has a soul. Everybody has some measure of goodness inside them."

There was usually some heated discussion on this point, as I recall.

"If I'm doing my job as your mom, then your heart will grow so big that you'll be able to find at least a tiny bit of space in it for every person in the world," I'd say. "You don't have to love everybody. But if you can start to feel your heart turning hard against someone, I hope you will try to find three good things you can say about that person."

We worked at it. When he was falling asleep at night, we'd talk about our day, and if he was having a hard time with someone in his life, we'd look for three good things we could say about the other person. Some days, he could only come up with one good thing to say about a person with whom he was struggling, and I'd offer some suggestions. He usually rejected any suggestions I made because they weren't his own ideas. We'd agree to try again the next time. (Baby steps, friends.)

It would have been easier to tell a different truth: Yes, son, I agree with you. Some people are monsters. There are people in the world who do not have your best interests at heart. Not everybody will be loving and loyal to you.

But you know what? He'd learned that, already, the hard way, at four years old. He didn't need me to reinforce it. He needed me to point him toward the light.

How much bitterness I had to swallow in those years. I'd

been told that I had to be superhuman, and there were a few moments when I think I maybe did the needful. I called on Duchess to help me. Duchess, who nurtured an evergreen love for all humanity. Duchess, who saw the spark of the divine in each person. My heart was brittle and broken, but Duchess stepped forward and put words of kindness and beauty in my mouth.

15

Now that the lightweights and barflies have cleared
out and I have the place to myself, I'd like to sing a few
numbers from my first album.

THE DUCHESS GOLDBLATT Dog Show started on my
birthday one year when I had nothing to do and nowhere
else to go. And then the Duchess Goldblatt Cat Show and its
popular spinoff, the Duchess Goldblatt Cat Show: Belly Divi-
sion, started — when? I can't remember. Whatever day it was,
I was both waving and drowning, desperately trying to keep
afloat. An online dog beauty pageant struck me funny. Duchess invited everyone to attend and reminded them that admission was free; they ought not purchase tickets from scalpers.

"How are you hosting a dog show?" asked Jackie, when I
told her about it.

"How am I not?"

"Where are you getting the pictures of all those dogs?"

"I'm not getting the pictures. People are posting pictures of their dogs to show me."

"And what do you do when they show you their dogs?"

"Nothing, really. I say nice things. I tell them their dogs are the glory of God incarnate and a joy to behold and so on, and then other people chime in and comment, too."

"And why are they doing this?"

I shrugged. "Why not? It's fun. Everybody likes sharing pictures of their pets. Besides, Duchess tells them to."

"You tell them to do stuff and they do it?"

"Yep."

"What else do you tell them to do?"

"Oh, you know, I tell them to do their best creative work, extend forgiveness to others, practice patience. It's the sort of thing my dad used to tell me to do, come to think of it. Most of the time when she tells them to do something, it's just me talking to myself. She uses her powers for good. Duchess gave them mindfulness assignments last year for springtime sacrifice during Lent."

"No, sir. You did not. You're making that up."

"Not at all. They took it very seriously."

"What did you make them give up?"

"I didn't *make* anybody do anything. Only the people who requested an assignment got one. Each person got something different. She suggested little sacrifices each person could consider making to help them practice mindfulness. You know, as a way to calm down and center your thinking."

"What kinds of sacrifices?"

"Don't look so frightened. It's not like I told anybody to go off their insulin. It was all tiny things that they wouldn't really suffer without, but they'd have to think about every day, like giving up wearing the color blue, maybe, or using exclamation points, or cooking with garlic. Or putting ice cubes in their drinks. I think I told someone that every time she used a pencil, she should pause for a moment and extend her heart in gratitude for the gifts she'd been given. That sort of thing."

"You told someone to give up ice cubes?"

"Yep. A guy in California."

"Did he do it?"

"Of course. No one would subvert Duchess's will. And a lot of people told me the things she chose for them to give up happened to be exactly the things they cared about. So somehow she picked the one little thing that would be meaningful."

> Someone has just reminded me that last year at this time, I gave out assignments for mindful sacrifice. Let me know if you need to re-up.

> *Whatcha got for me this year, your grace? — CT*

> Whenever you see the color purple, I'd like you to take a deep breath and hold it for a count of seven.

> *I could use your spiritual guidance, your grace. — D*

> I would like you to give up black pepper and, in so doing, pause for a moment's contemplation of the nature of suffering.

> *I'm on board. Let's do this. — E*

> I'd like you to give up basil, dearest, and in the moment you do, pause to forgive yourself.

> *I was just thinking of this today! Please bestow one upon me, your grace. — C*

I think I'd like you to give up sandwiches. Every time you forego, you will pause to remember one who has greatly loved you.

I am weak but the sourdough art strong. Still, I will try, your grace. — C

Ready and willing over here, too. — W

Whenever you see the color orange, you will find a kindness in your heart for your mother-in-law.

Tough one for me. — W

I know it is.

I'm ready for my sacrifice, your grace. Last year, it was silver jewelry, and if it were confession Tuesday, I'd admit it was hard. — P

I'd like you to stop using the word "very" and, in so doing, pause in contemplation of the gifts you've been given.

I need one, your grace. — AD

I'd like you to pick up and write with blue pens, not black pens or pencils. In so doing, contemplate what loving kindness means.

If you would, please, your grace. — BCD

Whenever you hear the word "trump," I'd like you to extend yourself in loving kindness to all who may not deserve it.

Now that is a challenge to rise to. Thank you, your grace. — BCD

I knew something was wrong as soon as Jackie called and I heard how sweet and cheerful her voice was. I'll tell you right now that Jackie calling me on purpose, wanting to talk to me in the middle of a weekday, is never a good sign.

"How's everything going?" she asked, her voice bright. "Having a nice day?"

Uh-oh. "What's wrong?"

"Nothing. Why would anything be wrong? No, I'm just curious if you'd like to explain why a giant box of pies has been FedExed to my home from a diner in Kansas," she said.

"Oh, that," I said, relieved. "That's for Duchess."

"No shit it's for Duchess," she said. "Who the hell else gets packages delivered to my house? I don't have room in my refrigerator for this."

"Seriously? You don't have room? How many pies did they send?"

She lowered her voice to the hiss she normally reserves for teenagers and dogs. "Get your ass over here and pick up these goddamned pies."

"Coming!" I said. (See, this is how I burn through the Man on the Outside couriers every six months. A lot of people don't have the patience for good, clean fun.)

I sailed out to her house, tickled to pieces. It turns out she did have room in her refrigerator for them (which I could have told you already; who can't make room for a couple of pies in an emergency?). She was sitting on the back steps, waiting for me.

"Oh, my God," she said, jumping up. "I almost couldn't wait for you to get here! You're not going to believe this. Wait until you see."

We opened the fridge and stood back, gazing at the beauty. Inside were two absolutely gorgeous sweet custard pies, each nestled in a golden crumb crust with a layer of homemade blackberry filling.

"Blackberry's my favorite," I told her. "How in the world did they know?"

"Magic," she said, taking one of the pies out. She sliced it up and we took our plates to the back porch, where we sat in reverent silence. Jackie was quiet for a long moment, her eyes closed, savoring each bite. "This is the best pie I've ever had."

She opened her eyes a crack. "Now, who the hell is sending you pies from Kansas?"

"It's a restaurant, the Ladybird Diner, in a city called Lawrence," I said. "I've seen pictures. It looks like a really special place. They love Duchess. They created a new pie recipe and named it specially after her."

"What? No," she said.

"Yep. They sure did," I said.

"Why would a diner in Kansas name a pie after Duchess Goldblatt?"

"I should think it would be obvious, Jackie. They love me. Let's go on a road trip. Let's visit!"

"A road trip to *Kansas?*" she said. "Do you have any idea how far Kansas is?"

"Yes." (No.) "Maybe next summer you'll take me? I've never been to Kansas."

"Of course you've never been to Kansas! It's a thousand miles away!"

"So this is the perfect opportunity," I said. "We'll take a road trip, have a little pie."

"I am not driving you to Kansas," she said. "Put the thought out of your mind. Also, forget about your other Duchess pie in my fridge. I'm keeping it."

"Absolutely," I said. "I'm sure our friends at the Ladybird Diner would want you to." She smiled. "You know what's really strange about all this with Duchess?" I asked her.

"Uh, yeah, I do, actually. Everything is strange about it," she said.

"No. Duchess remembers things, little details. My memory is gone, you know that. I don't remember anything."

"I've noticed."

"Duchess remembers people's pets' names, their kids' names, their spouses, what they do for a living, what they do for fun. I don't know how she's doing it."

"Are you trying to remember this stuff?"

"No. You know I don't remember anything. She remembers it without trying."

"Are you writing it down somewhere?"

"Come on. You know I don't care that much."

"That is very true," she said. "Remember that time you forgot my dog's name?"

"You've had so many dogs. I can't remember them all."

"I had one dog. One," she said. "The others had all been dead for at least five years, and you couldn't remember my one dog who was still alive. Sparkles! You knew Sparkles her whole life! She considered you part of her family!"

"My point," I said, "is that Duchess is somehow tapping into other parts of my brain to remember everything. Look through her list of people she's following." I handed over my phone. "Ask me about them."

"You're following six hundred people. How can you be following so many?"

"Well, they're not all talking at the same time. It's like being at a party. You move around and have different conversations. You mingle. And besides, I learn a lot from them.

You'd be surprised how funny and interesting people are. Okay. Go."

She started scrolling through the list, reading names out loud.

"I see here you've got a Shirley in California."

"She's one of Duchess's favorites. She used to be a realtor and now she's a personal trainer. She's got four or five kids, I think. All boys. She dressed up as Duchess one time. Hang on. I saved the picture."

"She dressed up as Duchess? What did she use for the hat and the ruff?"

"I don't know. I think she maybe made the ruff out of fabric or coffee filters," I said. "Here. Look." I took the phone and found the picture of California Shirley I'd saved.

"Jesus Christ," Jackie said. "She's wearing coffee filters."

"Isn't she adorable?"

"She's beautiful," Jackie said. "All right, let's see who else is in here. Benjamin Dreyer?"

"Love him. He's in New York. He's become a real friend."

"What do you mean, *real?* You've met him?"

"No, of course not. I mean we've shared the deepest truths of our hearts with one another. Although he has been writing a book for a few years now, maybe four or five years, and Duchess has told him when the book comes out, if he has a party, she'll come to life for him."

"How is she going to come to life and go to his party?"

"Me. I mean me. I would go to his party."

"You're going to leave the house, leave town, go to New York City, and go to a publishing party? How are you going to introduce yourself?"

I paused. It was possible I hadn't thought all this through. "I'll think of something. Don't worry about it. Anyway,

Benjamin promised his partner that when he finished the manuscript, they could finally get a dog, and the dog they adopted seems so sweet. Sallie. Kind of a pittie mix, I think, white with reddish-brown spots. Everyone's smitten with Sallie."

"Okay. Adam."

"Which one? She's got a couple of Adams. Oh, yes, Adam Begley. He's in England. He's got this wonderful huge, shaggy, salt-and-peppery sort of dog named Olive. A wolfhound of some sort, maybe? I ought to know the breed. Give me my phone. I'll message him."

"On your own time," she said, leaning away and holding my phone out of my reach. "Good Maggie."

"Good Maggie! Duchess calls her Goodness. She's a children's librarian. She has two dogs, although I think the dogs live with her parents. Bentley's sort of a golden retriever, maybe, and Elphaba, I don't know what kind of dog. Kind of a pointy-eared white dog. When she got married, she and her husband held up a giant portrait of Duchess between them at the wedding."

"No."

"Oh, yes. Her mother had it printed up and framed. Took it with her for the wedding. Duchess was invited to the wedding, as a matter of fact."

"What? These people invited you to their wedding?"

"No, not me. They invited Duchess. She said she would have gone, too, but only if they'd let her officiate."

"I can't believe the mother of the bride brought a portrait of Duchess to her daughter's wedding."

"She handmade Duchess Goldblatt Christmas ornaments one year, too."

"We'll come back to that. Cedar Waxwing."

"Oh, Cedar Waxwing. Duchess told him to use that name for some reason. I forget why. His real name is Nate. He's a software developer in Boston. He has a cat named Ted, and he sends Ted's pictures in to the Duchess Goldblatt Cat Show. He made me a video on New Year's Eve saying 'Happy New Year' with Ted."

"You have a cat show? Don't answer that. I'm still thinking about the wedding and the Christmas ornaments. Let's keep going. Howard Mittelmark."

"Howard's a wonderful writer and editor. She loves him. He reads Duchess very carefully. He, more than anybody, can tell when I'm struggling and the sadness comes through in Duchess's voice, and he'll send me a private message to check in on me and make sure I'm okay. She considers him one of her dear ones. No pets, as far as I know."

"Connie Schultz."

"Oh, yes. The columnist. Journalist. She's married to Sherrod Brown."

"I don't know who that is," she said.

"Senator from Ohio. They have a long-haired dachshund mix, I think, named Franklin. You know those silky long-haired dachshunds who are sort of a dark brown and black and they have those big beautiful brown eyes?"

"Are you telling me there's a senator who knows about Duchess Goldblatt?"

"I should certainly hope so. If anybody needs to benefit from the bright shining light and wisdom of the universe that Duchess embodies, it's the US government."

"Right. Let me ask you this," she said, putting the phone down. "What's my job?"

I paused for a minute. "You're kind of like a social worker," I said.

"A social worker?" she repeated.

"No? A manager of social workers. You're a manager."

She glared at me.

"Of course not," I said. "No, I know that's wrong. Director of development. A grant writer? You're a grant writer. You used to be a social worker, though, right?"

"You are unbelievable."

"I'm sorry," I said. "I can't help it. I'm not doing it on purpose."

"It makes no sense," she said. "How are you remembering all these details about people you don't even know?"

"I have no idea," I told her. "Although it does kind of feel like I know them."

"They don't know you. They're not your real friends. They don't even know your name."

"They know my heart," I said. "They know my voice. Those are the best parts of me. I never really liked my name anyway, to be honest with you. You know what's funny, come to think of it? I used to have an incredible memory. It was freakish. I could recognize people from having been on the same bus with them five years before. I could hold a whole book in my head and see every part of it at once. I've lost so much ground, but it's almost like Duchess has found a path back to my memory. She's turned the lights back on."

"If Duchess is able to form new memories, then your memory is still there. Why do you think you're forgetting so much?"

"I don't know, but I'll tell you what: it's a relief. If I run into someone I used to know, and I can't recall their name or their parents' names or every way they ever let me down, all I think is: thank God. I thank God for taking my memory away. Losing my memories can only be good for me."

All lost manuscripts have since been found, numbered, bathed in rose water, and shredded for confetti. It's what they would have wanted.

16

You may wonder how a small non-existent town in New York can afford expanded services and a Vodka Festival. Grants and peep shows, mostly.

*D*ID I MENTION I got promoted? I lead a team of fifteen people now, God help them. It's the kind of work I enjoy, because it requires encouraging people, which is kind of my jam, but then there's a fair amount of routine paperwork that only takes about half a dozen working brain cells and a spreadsheet. Sometimes on the nights when my son is with his dad, I'll be reviewing people's expense reports or approving their paid time-off requests, and I'm using only part of the old noggin. You know how it is when the rest of your brain goes prancing out and about in the world making friends without you. This is the kind of thing that I find she's been up to while I'm not looking.

Let me just set this here to remind you that truth and beauty are still with us, and goodness is all around.

Sometimes it's difficult to see it. — B

I know it is.

Thank you, your grace. I feel total despair, but I will try to remember all that is good. — N

On the whole, I think we're moving toward enlightenment, sweets.

Everything feels so insidious. Democracy, discourse, civility, empathy, all crumbling. — N

Chin up, poodle. I raised you to be fearlessly Goldblattian. Draw on it now.

You never disappoint. — D

I think I'll have that on my tombstone, if you don't mind.

You could, if you were mortal. — D

Thank you, your grace. Forgive me, it's 3 a.m. I'm on west coast awaiting red-eye flight. Love trumps hate. — M

> You may talk to me at 3 a.m. if you like. I am usually up and about anyway.

"Uneasy lies the head that wears a crown" and that is why we as your subjects sleep soundly and in quiet assurance. — M

You are our anchor, your grace. — N

You've got your work cut out for you, your grace. — E

> Lean hard with me on the side of sweetness and light, and we can rock it over.

This is an excellent and noble challenge, madam, and I accept. You are a bright star in our murky world today. — E

Duchess, you are a beacon of civility in an uncivil world. We thank you! — ME

> Thank you for your kind words, sweets. I'm glad to see you here.

Thank you for this timely reminder, your grace. — D

Thank you, your grace. We need you tonight. — M

You have no idea how much I needed this just now, your grace. Or maybe you do. — X

17

Food trucks never caught on in Crooked Path. We have advice trucks. People like to run out at noon and grab five minutes with a Jungian.

M Y VOICE, IT may surprise you to find out, I have on occasion hoarded to myself. I understood intuitively as a small child that my voice was a gift — not a gift in the sense of a talent, but a gift because it was divinely given, just like anybody else's: the voice is the mingling of the soul, the mind, and the body together, expressed through breath, which is life itself; how could any human voice not be sacred? I saw clearly that no one could demand a share of it. It was absolutely mine.

In childhood, I didn't speak at all until I was three or four — a fact that no one thought to mention to me until I was an adult, and then only as an afterthought — and I didn't speak outside the home until I was around nine. I can remember an elderly religious teacher standing over me, screaming at me to obey, to answer when spoken to. Speak!

The request was fundamentally unjust, and I rejected it as such. I'd sized her up early on when she gave a lecture on despair that I've never forgotten. Despair is an unforgivable sin, she'd claimed; it means you've chosen to give up on God. Not even God can ever forgive a suicide, she told us. He couldn't forgive it even if he *wanted* to, and he wouldn't ever want to. A suicide will never get into heaven, ever.

I didn't make eye contact with her. I wouldn't give her the satisfaction. I kept my eyes down, but I heard every word she said, and I knew she was dead wrong. I knew in my bones, had always known, that my brother would eventually commit suicide, I knew he was a child of God just as much as anybody else, and I knew that when he died he would be welcomed into heaven. If she'd ever seen despair up close, she would know what I knew, that God understands the nature of a broken heart. The saddest people will always be allowed to go home first.

I didn't have the vocabulary to articulate this in the first grade, but the truth of it was fully clear to me. She didn't speak for God. She had missed the whole point of God's love. She misunderstood the nature of the divine and was, therefore, not to be trusted. She had no right to tell me anything or to demand a share in my voice. I can remember retreating into my mind to calm myself. I pictured the very center of my being as a black iron bar, vertically positioned at the center of my eternal spirit. I imagined myself holding on to it with both hands for support. Whatever happened, I retreated ever further inward and held on. Things around me were not okay, but I was okay, as long as I stayed inside myself and held on. I never told anyone else about her words, either; my father, in particular, had to be protected from the hateful things she had said about suicidal people. Even then, his heart was not as strong as mine, and as long as he lived, I never repeated it to him.

And no matter what she ever did or said or threatened me with, I never, ever once spoke to her.

That teacher called my father in to discuss my refusal to speak. "No one at this school has ever heard the child speak," she said. "We're not convinced the child *can* speak."

"What child?" my father said. "Mine? Well, sure, she's a little shy with new people, but she's incredibly verbally gifted. Have you seen her writing? She writes stories and plays. She wrote a novel and printed it herself. She hand-sewed the binding. She makes up characters. She sings all day. She never stops talking."

My father brought it up to me later at home, lifting me up to sit on the kitchen counter where he could look me in the eye and discuss it.

"Your teacher seems to be of the opinion that you don't know how to talk."

I shrugged. "I'm sure my teacher's opinions are none of my business."

"Quite so, quite so. And so would you say you do talk at school?"

"No."

"Do you think you might start talking at school sometime?"

"No."

He nodded. "All right, sweetheart," he said. He lifted me off the counter and set me back down on the floor. "I know when you're ready to use your voice, you will."

As an adult, I'm aware there's a name for the phenomenon of a child who can speak in some circumstances but not others. It's an anxiety disorder called selective mutism. I remember exactly what it felt like: I could not speak, even when I tried. My mouth refused to open, no sound would come out, no matter what I did. The muscles couldn't be moved any more than I could move a chair across the room with my mind. My only option was to retreat into the deep peace of silence. I didn't look at people straight on. I kept my face smooth and still like a statue. But I listened, and inside my mind, I took notes.

I'm also aware of a quote often attributed to Freud: "All family life is organized around the most damaged person in it." I wasn't even standing near the front of that line. In my family, in my home, in the time and the circumstances in which I was raised, anyone who could do nine years without speaking outside the family was a champ and a blessing and a bullet dodged, not a problem to be solved.

I've drawn a line down the page here, in invisible ink, between the part of the story that's mine to tell and that which belongs to other people, both the living and the dead.

> I put my ear to the ground over here and over there.
> I have to if I want to see how the pieces of the world
> fit together.

Duchess:

It would be so great to see you again, if you could be there. And please bring whomever you'd like. I'd be happy to have you as my guests. Thank you for all your support on social media. Duchess continues to entertain and amaze me.

Yours, Lyle

Hello, Rascal —

I would love to come see you! SUPER EXCITING!
THANK YOU, LYLE! Duchess sends all best —

That is such great news! Would you be willing to come a
little early so we could visit? Are your numerous followers in that city a coincidence, or have folks there figured
it out? Please return my best wishes to Duchess. — Lyle

Every time I've gone to see Lyle, he has always invited me to
bring along a friend. Well, who would you bring? With whom
would you share your rarest and most precious gift? No one
I knew deserved it, and I hinted at that truth to him as deli-
cately as I could.

"No one I know deserves it," I'd tell him.

He'd laugh.

I went to see him once in an acoustic show in which he
shared the stage with John Hiatt. I'd seen them perform several times together previously, years before I ever imagined I
might meet Lyle in person. Lyle told me that John Hiatt would
pose no problem from the Duchess-secret-keeping point of
view; Hiatt wasn't much for socializing with strangers after the show and wouldn't bump into me. Lyle's manager already knew me, and Lyle introduced me to some of the other
musicians and people who worked behind the scenes for the
show, but they didn't bat an eye; Lyle knew people all over the
world, after all. They didn't think anything of someone hanging around with him backstage.

There was only one hitch. Another friend of Lyle's would
be coming to the same show. How would we explain how
we knew each other without mentioning Duchess Goldblatt?

Lyle and I spoke on the phone in advance, and we tried to hatch a plan.

He told me his friend's name, but added, "We call him 'the Genius.'"

"That sounds ominous," I said.

"He's great. You'll like him." He went on to describe the Genius's work, which had something to do with sound editing and isolating one sound in a live televised performance through a mic, one voice or one instrument, and using algorithms somehow to correct the pitch. I vaguely understood only a fraction of it. "We're thinking maybe you can tell him you're an old friend of April's somehow."

"I think we want to be careful," I said. "We can't start lying to protect Duchess. We can't let her railroad us into being deceptive to keep her secrets."

"You're just too ethical," he said.

"We have to be firm with Duchess, Lyle," I said. "We have to maintain clear boundaries, or she'll walk all over us."

"I'll leave this up to you. It's your thing. However you want to handle it, I'll follow your lead."

"Well, we're not going to lie for her. It's important to me not to lie," I said. "You know what? I'll just tell your friend the Genius the truth. The truth is always the best bet. I'll tell him it's a secret, and that'll be the end of it."

"Sure. Whatever you think," Lyle said.

So I did meet the Genius, and he was absolutely lovely, a delight. We visited together before the show, the three of us.

"Let me ask you this, Lyle," I said. "How do you see ideas taking shape in your mind? Do you see a piece of paper with the story written on it?"

He made a face. "What do you mean, how do I see ideas? I don't know. They're just ideas."

"I see a piece of paper in my mind, all the time, with words on it," I said. I asked the Genius the same question.

"I don't see words, but I know what you mean. I see geometry everywhere," he said. "I see dimensions. Patterns. Lines, angles, distance between objects in the room. The intersections of lines. When I hear music, I can see it as geometrical patterns."

"I think I read once that's how Beethoven's mind worked," I said. "He could visualize music."

Lyle glanced back and forth between the two of us.

"What?" I said.

"No. Nothing," he said.

Later that night, when he was onstage in the acoustic show, he turned to John Hiatt. They always keep a friendly patter going between songs in their concerts. Lyle paused at one point, tuned his guitar for a long moment, and then deadpanned, "John, let me ask you. How do you see ideas forming in your mind? Do you see a piece of paper with a story written on it" — he held up his hands and waved them around — "or do you visualize music in equations and dimensions?"

The audience laughed along at the oddity of it, and Hiatt gave it a little thought and went on to answer. But I don't know what John Hiatt said because the Genius and I were laughing too hard to hear it.

"So how did you come to know Lyle again?" the Genius asked me.

"We're friends," I said, thinking: There! Friends! That should settle it.

"Uh-huh. Friends. So you must know April."

"Well, no. Sort of. I mean, of course I know *of* April. We haven't met. She knows who I am."

That sounded sketchy even to my ears. Usually I don't

mind the tactical deployment of a quick cold shoulder to end an unwanted conversation, but we were both Lyle's invited guests. I couldn't bear to appear rude to any friend of his. I had to try to explain myself.

"All right, listen," I said. "I can't tell you. It's a secret. But April knows it's a secret. It's cool."

"What do you mean, it's a *secret?* It's not a secret."

I hadn't counted on the very validity of my secret being questioned. How can you talk to someone who doesn't let you keep a secret? What do you do with a person who doesn't respect the sacred boundaries of singer-fan confidentiality?

"You're friends with Lyle but you don't know April?" he said. "How'd you manage that?"

I started to panic. How could I explain that this was innocence itself? I was a fictional character, that's all; I wrote online in the voice of an elderly author who considered herself a literary superstar. Nothing to see here. Move along, pal.

Somehow I hemmed and hawed and dodged and weaved until after the show when we met up with Lyle again, and I took him aside and whispered, "I'm getting nervous, man. Your buddy's asking a lot of questions. He's not respecting the sanctity of the secret."

Lyle said quietly, "Well, you handle this however you think is right. I won't say anything. Tell him whatever you want. Or don't tell him anything."

"I'm not telling him anything! I can't have people asking all these questions. She'll kill me. Plus, I know he doesn't really care, and this secret does mean something to me. It's important to me."

Lyle nodded. "I understand. I trust your judgment. Do what you think is best."

So I resolved to say nothing and I thought that was the end of it, but here's where I miscalculated: the Genius was no regular person. He was an engineer. An engineer, of all things! It's supposed to be that once you say it's a secret, boom: that's the end. No more questions. You're talking to an architect, a dog groomer, an English professor, bartender, that's it. Show's over. End of conversation. You don't have to go home, but you can't stay here.

But an engineer! My God. They want to solve every puzzle they find. He kept after me, asking questions.

We were sitting around late that night, after the show, visiting. I was sitting next to Lyle, trying to take a selfie of Lyle and me without getting myself in it at all — I didn't want a picture of me, just Lyle; what do I need with a picture of myself? Lyle said, "But if you're not in it, it's not a selfie; that's the whole point of a selfie —"

"So how is it that you two know each other?" the Genius asked again.

I glanced sidelong at Lyle. He was completely stone-faced. He kept his eyes dead-even on the Genius and stayed silent. He didn't glance to the left or right, didn't give an inch. True to his word, he left it up to me. Now that's a real friend right there, folks.

"Okay, fine. I'll tell you," I said. "But you can't tell anybody." I took a deep breath. "I have a social media account. I write under a made-up name. And Lyle likes to read what I write."

"Oh. I see," said the Genius.

And there: that was it. Once he knew the secret, he lost interest. We went on to talk about other things, but in the back of my mind, I knew Duchess was displeased with me. Once again, I'd given away something that was precious to me to someone who didn't care about it at all.

Crack yourself open 45 degrees at the waist and see
if there's another, smaller you inside. That might be
the real one.

Later on, maybe around midnight, we were still sitting around
chatting and I realized I ought to get going. I still had to drive
a few hours to get home. I started to think about making my
way back to my car, and I realized, with more than a little
panic, that I had no idea where I'd left it.

I'd been so excited to get to the show that I'd parked about
three blocks away, on the street, and figured, as one does, that
I'd find my way back later. It was a small town. I hadn't walked
too far, a block or two in one direction and then I'd turned the
corner and walked a block more to reach the theater. How far
off could I be?

The important thing now, I figured, was not to let on that
I'd forgotten where I put my car. Normal people do not lose
all their most important things, like their cars and houses and
families and husbands and friends.

Plus, Lyle had the idea I was smart. I hated to spoil that
for him.

I stood up and said my good-nights to Lyle, to the Genius,
to his manager, to Lyle's bodyguard. He might not have been
a bodyguard. I can't quite place who he was. I think there was
a fourth man there, but I can't remember for sure, to be honest with you. Maybe there were only three guys there. I'm not
Robert Caro, for Christ's sake.

"Well, so long," I said, leaping up and heading for the door.
Two more steps and I'm out the door, I thought, and then I'm
home free.

"We'll walk you to your car," Lyle said, standing up.

"No, no, no, no need," I said. "I parked super close. Don't
worry about it. Good night!"

"We're going to walk you to your car," Lyle said.

"Please don't trouble yourself. Totally unnecessary."

"We're from Texas," Lyle said, opening the door for me. "We're the kind of guys who are going to walk you to your car."

Uh-oh. "The thing is" — I sighed — "I'm not exactly sure where I left it. I think I'll just take a little walk until I find it."

"Fine," Lyle said. "We're going with you."

So we walked a block this way and a block that way; two blocks this way, a block over that way, a block back. Nothing looked familiar. It was a smallish town, home to a university and maybe one good coffee shop. I knew I hadn't started out all that far away. How hard could it be to find a car?

We kept walking until we found it on a dark side street, sometime after midnight, and stood there saying our goodbyes. Just then a joyful young college man, having been celebrating his youth and the warmth of a fine May evening with a generous helping of spirits, came rolling down a flight of stairs, through an open door, and onto the sidewalk in front of us. He rolled on the ground in front of Lyle and gaped, slack-jawed, as slow understanding dawned in his glazed, bloodshot eyes: he took in every detail, from the custom-made cowboy boots to the beautifully cut suit, to the pocket square, to the tie, to the famous grin — to the man who would be absolutely recognizable on any street corner anywhere in the world, I imagine, even to a drunken college kid falling down the stairs.

"Holy shit," the fellow said, looking up from his position sprawled on the sidewalk.

"Howdy," said Lyle, extending his hand to help him up.

"I know you!" the young man said, wobbling under the streetlight. "Jesus Christ!"

What a story you'll have to tell tomorrow if you remember, I thought, watching the young man stumble back up the stairs.

Of course, I'll tell it better.

18

New Year's Eve, steam the new year in a pot of water with a bay leaf. Any months that don't open on their own are no good. Throw them out.

As a small child, I recognized that I had a calling in life. No one ever told me this was the case, but in the way that very young children can perceive the truth of the things happening around them without being able yet to articulate the reasons, I saw clearly: my father's heart was breaking, and it was my job to lift his spirits. And I could do it, a tiny bit at a time, by making him laugh. Once I saw that I could do it, I had to do it.

I wanted to get him going with a deep rolling belly laugh. That was always the goal. Once or twice in my life, I made him laugh until he cried. In my mind, in my heart, I can still hear him laughing. That was the brass ring: my life's work, and I knew it at five years old, at seven, at ten. I didn't speak in public, but I watched everything and took notes inside my head;

walking home from school, I would parse the day's events in my mind, turning them over and over to find a few promising strands I could weave into a story. Funny ideas are everywhere if you're vigilant and always on the lookout, as I had to be. School and playmates were fleeting and irrelevant distractions from my real work, which went on in my head. I paced my stories out every afternoon, walking home, a miniature Wallace Stevens on his lunch hour.

I found there was a certain tone I could hit that played well with my target audience. He liked good-natured humor, kind humor that didn't hurt anyone; a clever play on words or the surprise punch line he couldn't see coming. Like many lovers of the written word, he delighted in wit, and he was an appreciative connoisseur of careful cursing; he understood its power. From him I learned comic timing, the effect of the right word deployed in the right moment.

I never understood the appeal of bothering to be the class clown or of wasting my talents on the kids at school. Who cared about the kids at school? I didn't even notice them. He was my audience. He was my whole heart. In my mind, the stakes for my work couldn't have been higher, and his was the only opinion that ever mattered.

> The metaphorical ledges in Crooked Path are all built in compliance with Eurocode, Chicago building code, and Strunk & White's *Elements.*

There was another time I met one of Lyle's friends, and this one was a little bit easier, at least in the sense that Lyle told me in advance he wouldn't ask questions. It was the singer-songwriter Robert Earl Keen.

Now, I'd known of Robert Earl Keen for years and years, ever since Lyle included his name in his song "Record Lady"

("Robert Earl is a friend of mine / You know he's always looking after my best interests"), so I knew his music and I was delighted to see him perform, but I was even more interested to watch him and Lyle together. If you're a lifelong practitioner of the eavesdropping arts, as I fancy myself, you enjoy nothing better than to listen to two old friends talk and tell stories.

We visited before the show and after the show, and then later Lyle and I were standing outside on the corner when a couple came out of the theater and walked past. They stopped and stared at Lyle for a minute before approaching cautiously and asking for a picture. He posed with them, asked their names, shook their hands, and thanked them for coming to the show.

"I'm shaking," the man said to me, as he and his partner stepped away. "My hands are shaking. I can't believe it. I've been a fan for so long. I never, ever imagined I might get to meet him."

"I know," I said, catching his excitement, and we laughed together at the sudden joy of it. I knew exactly what he meant.

> I keep a silver bowl full of emails by the front door.
> Anyone who tries to pop in for a visit has to take a bag of them for the ride home.

Most of the time I didn't take anyone with me to Lyle's shows, but I made one exception. He was at one point planning a trip close to my home, bringing April with him, and planning to perform along with his Large Band and a regional gospel choir. Another well-known musician would be performing before them.

I thought it would be a perfect time to let Jackie tag along, and I told Lyle she'd be joining me.

Lyle called me a few days in advance.

"April and I need to know what we can say to Jackie," he said. "Can we mention Duchess? Does she know about Duchess?"

"Oh, yeah," I said. "She knows all about Duchess, but she doesn't care. She's of the opinion she gets plenty enough of me already. She's not necessarily looking for more. She doesn't even bother reading Duchess, if you can imagine such lunacy."

It is true that my dear friend Jackie, whom I had raised from a pup, adores me in sort of a limited way, in small doses, as it were, and although she wasn't interested in my alter ego, she was thrilled to pieces to get to meet Lyle and April. Who could blame her?

I prepared her for the special experience as gently as possible.

"Stay out of the way or I'll kill you," I said.

She nodded. "That feels fair."

We were standing around at the back of the concert hall, waiting for Lyle and April to arrive, and there were a number of people milling about: venue workers, technicians, security. The gospel choir was in a large room with the door open, rehearsing. We could see through giant floor-to-ceiling windows the back lot where the tour buses would be arriving. Lyle texted me that they were about fifteen minutes away, so Jackie and I were standing around, waiting, when the doors opened and a little tan-and-black dog came prancing in. I'm not great with breeds, but I thought he had the intelligent eyes and spiky hairlike fur of a terrier. There might have been a couple of people accompanying the dog; I don't know. I only had eyes for him, and he scooted over to say hello to me.

"Hello, sweet love," I said to the dog, clapping my hands for him to come to me.

A woman, possibly the dog's owner or possibly a friend of his owner, followed him over to retrieve him.

"Would you just look at this sweet little fellow!" I said to Jackie.

Jackie didn't say anything, but she slipped her hand behind me and surreptitiously dug her nails into the small of my back.

"Cut it out," I said, swatting her hand away. "Look at his little face! Hello, sweetheart!" I said to the dog. "He's so adorable I can't stand it," I told the woman. She was strikingly pretty, her silvery white hair pulled away from her face. She smiled and said hello before guiding the dog away.

Jackie leaned in toward my ear as the woman retreated.

"You dumb motherfucker. That was Emmylou Harris," she hissed.

"You know I'm not great with faces," I said.

"How do you not recognize Emmylou Harris backstage at an Emmylou Harris concert!"

Well, as I say: I'm not always 100% paying attention. It's possible I may have missed a few things along the way.

> Let's ask ourselves if our desired outcomes are in alignment with our behaviors. My wineglass isn't refilling itself, folks.

"What's for dinner?" my son asked.

"Hang on, honey," I said. "Give me two seconds."

"What are you doing?" He peeked over my shoulder. "Are you still being Bladder Gus on Vine?"

I sighed. "It's not Bladder Gus on Vine. It's Duchess Goldblatt on Twitter. And yes. The good people of the world need my wisdom and counsel."

He shook his head, the wise old soul. "Being Duchess Goldblatt isn't going to help your gaming skills, Mommy."

"That is one hundred percent true," I said. "And yet I get such a kick out of it that I stubbornly refuse to quit."

> Back from touring the lake district in my Mercedes
> pinewood derby S550. It gets great gas mileage;
> never mind what "Consumer Reports" says.

"So what are you going to do with Duchess?" Lyle asked me on the phone one day.

"I think a book," I said. "I'm working on a book. I can see it, in my mind, coming together in fragments. I have all these little broken pieces that I think I can put together to form a new pattern. It's like a mosaic."

"A book, sure. But I think more than that. The world needs this story of how you're using your talents as a force for good. It's that universal love you foster. That universal acceptance you're offering people, the community you're creating. This is why people go to church: to pray together in community. Otherwise we could just stay home and pray alone. You're like Jesus that way," he added with a chuckle.

I knew he was pulling my leg there; Lyle is a serious churchgoing man who sings with his church choir. But still.

"I'd die before asking you to change one hair on your head, but I need you to not tell me I'm Jesus," I said. "I admit to you privately that I find it a little overwhelming."

"I don't mean to overwhelm you. I'm trying to be encouraging."

"That you are," I said. "Nobody has ever encouraged me as much as you do."

"I'll call my publicist," Lyle said. "I think you should be on *CBS Sunday Morning*. April and I love that show. We always try to see it. And it's not just you, you know, it's the people you've brought together. That's the story. Everyone needs to hear Duchess's story."

"No, no, no." I started to panic. "Don't call anybody. Don't tell anybody anything."

"Okay. When you're ready. Did I ever talk to you about my friend —" He mentioned a name I'd never heard.

"No. What was his name?"

He repeated it. "He made a film about Robert Rauschenberg you might have seen, and he was a director at the Guggenheim."

"No. I don't think you did. I think I'd remember that name."

Lyle went on to tell me about his friend, who has had quite a career but is also a motorcycle fancier who curated a show about the art of the motorcycle, I think Lyle said, for the Guggenheim, and Lyle — as you may know, if you're a fan of Lyle's, and why wouldn't you be — is also a motorcycle enthusiast, and maybe that's how they became friends, but I can't remember because I was at that moment getting distracted thinking about the friend's first name, and whether I had heard it wrong, but I thought it was an Irish name, which would make sense because the last name was Irish. This reminded me of my late grandmother, who had an aesthetic preference for first names that matched their last names: German last name, German first name; Irish last name, Irish first name, and so on. I used to babysit for a girl named something like Maeve Agostinelli, which I thought was beautiful, but it was fingernails on a blackboard to my poor grandmother, who liked everything to match. Not me. I subscribe to a more Dickensian position. "There are dark shadows on the earth," wrote Dickens, "but its lights are stronger in the contrast."

"How do you spell his name?" I interrupted Lyle.

"U-l-t-a-n," he said.

"Irish. Thought so. Okay. Go on."

"He's not on social media at all, but I was telling Ultan he ought to be on social media just for this character, Duchess Goldblatt."

"Uh-huh."

"And he said, Oh, yes, he's heard of Duchess Gold-blatt."

"How is that possible?" I said. "He was being polite to you, that's all."

"Oh, no. He knows what's going on. He's very well connected in the art world," Lyle said.

"I don't doubt that at all. I'm sure he's well connected, but I'm not," I said.

"People know Duchess," Lyle said. "Your reach is incredible."

"No! There are book critics who follow her, but I can't imagine they sit around and talk about her. Who would have told him about Duchess if it wasn't you? This is the damnedest thing I ever heard," I said.

"Write your book," said Lyle. "If you don't write your book, I'm going to write it."

"Good. Do it. I'll take a nap. Maybe I'll go see a movie."

"You write your book yourself."

"Well, you'll have to read it before anyone else does," I said.

"And I will be very honored, whenever you're ready to share," Lyle said.

"How's Lyle?" Duchess's friend Benjamin Dreyer asked her via private message.

"He's good. I asked him to stop telling me I'm Jesus."

"That seems reasonable."

> Everyone, at one time or another, requires an encouraging Goldblattian whisper in the ear. Great things are coming, friends. I can feel it.

I need one, please! — KL

> Hello, sunshine of my life. Everything you need to do, you can do, and I believe that you will. All will be well, love.

Thank you, DG, for this and for everything. — KL

"Sign here and here," I said to Jackie, sliding a paper to her across the dinner table.

"What's that?" asked my son.

"It's a confidentiality agreement," I said. "Jackie's agreeing she won't tell anyone I'm Duchess Goldblatt."

"Should I sign one, too?" he asked.

"There's no need, honey," I said. "Minors can't enter into contracts on their own."

"I like to be included," he said.

"Okay, you can sign one, too," I said.

He took the document from me carefully, with both hands, but then paused before signing.

"What if my teacher says I'll get detention if I don't tell her who Duchess Goldblatt is?"

"That would be unreasonable and unjust."

"But what if she did it anyway?"

"We'd fight it. We'd go all the way to the Board of Education if we had to."

He smiled. "I was kidding. I know she won't ask. Besides, I won't ever tell anyone. Ever. Your secret is safe with me."

There had been a day, a few months before this, when I'd visited his school. I'd been standing amongst a group of parents and children, all milling around, and a woman in front of me heard me say my son's name. She whirled around to face me and touched my arm.

"Are you his mother?" she asked. "I was hoping to meet you. I'm his math teacher."

I took her hand, a little wary. It was the sort of conversation opener that could go either way, what with the state's forced emphasis on standardized testing, which all the research says is not necessarily an effective measure of learning, and the new standards, which in my opinion are —

"He is a beautiful human being," the teacher said, her eyes bright. "Just a beautiful soul. I'm so glad I got a chance to tell you that."

Once more, a sound moved through sudden rightnesses. I knew for sure that he was going to be all right because in that moment I saw it written on my bones.

And finally, with that, I could breathe.

> I have never described to you what Hacienda looks like, and yet I almost think you might know.

19

Save on entertaining expenses by keeping up with only one friend, ideally a fictional person who prefers not to leave the house.

*I*N SMALL BITS and pieces, here and there, Duchess began to correspond by private message with PJ in Galveston, the one who liked to carry around a laminated picture of Duchess and take selfies with it. It was more than that: PJ had coffee mugs made up with Duchess's picture on them and shipped them around the country to other friends of Duchess Goldblatt. She had Duchess Goldblatt T-shirts and bookmarks and Christmas stockings made. She posted a photo of her Duchess coffee mug every morning, or sometimes two Duchess coffee mugs. At one point, PJ decided to attend a Lyle Lovett and Robert Earl Keen concert, at which she was able to meet them after the show and she presented them both with, of course, their own Duchess Goldblatt mugs.

I don't really remember how we started corresponding. At what moment is a friendship conceived? When does it become a viable form of life?

PJ: Vodka soda on the rocks with a splash of cranberry juice and I am reborn. I had two but I wanted five. It was so hot out and just the very thing. — DG

Fresh! Hydrating! I admire your ability to have two. — PJ

Now I'm thinking cutting my own hair is a great idea. — DG

Step away from the scissors. — PJ

How hard can it be? — DG

No. No no no. It's hard. — PJ

Listen. Hear me out. I pull it back in a low pony and snip. — DG

No. — PJ

> Lucy and Ethel could have been happy. Ethel could've run the building; Lucy could've been a bandleader. It would have been a good life.

One summer night, Lyle was planning a concert in Westchester County, New York, and two of Duchess's friends both mentioned to Duchess separately by private message that they planned to attend the show, so I told Lyle they'd be there.

He called me a week in advance to tell me he'd priced out

having a giant image of Duchess projected onto the stage prior to the show.

"Oh, my God," I said. "You did not."

"I did," he said. "But the theater's a union shop, the employees are all union, so the cost of having a projectionist show the image of Duchess onstage would be four thousand dollars. I said, Man, I love Duchess, but four thousand bucks!"

"Duchess says she can't imagine any possible better use of four thousand dollars, Lyle," I said.

"I told April we've got to get you here for the show," he said. "Come on. Let's get you on a plane."

"I'm not going to get on a plane. I'm afraid to fly."

"Then we'll send a car. I have this vision of you standing backstage and getting to meet your fans. They're really nice people. I promise you'd like them."

"I don't doubt it. I'm sure they're wonderful," I said. "But I can't meet them. It would be the end of Duchess."

They will only end up leaving me: I saw that thought creeping around the corner and I kicked it away inside my mind, but I knew it was still there. It would come sneaking in again later, probably after dark.

"Well, one day you're going to meet them, when you're ready," he said. "And it's going to be great."

> You can take your feelings out to thaw, but figure
> 30 minutes per pound in the fridge. Don't leave them in
> the sink. They'll grow spores.

"How do you have time for this?" my cousin Annie asked me once, scrolling through Duchess's conversations on my phone. "The back-and-forth is so fast. I can't even keep up with her."

"I just check in quick while I'm doing other stuff," I said. "Maybe I'm in line at the store, or waiting for a meeting to start, that kind of thing. I take two minutes to be Duchess, and then I go back to whatever else I was doing."

"Doesn't it interfere with work?"

"No," I said. "If anything, it's making my work better."

"Aren't you expected to produce a lot in your job, though?"

"Yeah, but I do. I could take a week off every month and still outperform the goals they set for me."

"Come on. You have a hard job. How are you doing that?" Annie asked me.

"I don't know," I said. "I think somehow Duchess is making me smarter."

"Seriously?"

"Yeah. She's definitely making me a better writer. Let's say I'm consciously working on a hard problem at work, and I look away from it and play around with being Duchess for a few minutes. Then when I go back to my problem with fresh eyes, I can solve it. I'll give you an example: Let's say I'm tired of working and getting burned out. Duchess is thinking about Möbius strips and strip malls and thinking about the intersections between those two ideas, and what might be funny about that. It's kind of like playing with a Rubik's Cube while you're trying to solve an equation."

"What are Möbius strips?"

"A rectangle that's been twisted and joined at the ends to make a loop. It turns around on itself so you can't say which part of the circle is the inside track and which part is the outside. So she's thinking, you know, a Möbius strip–slash–strip mall, right: it would be one of those old dying suburban malls shaped like a Möbius strip, an infinite twisted loop. So maybe her town planned to tear down an old strip mall, but because it's a Möbius strip mall, the demolition crew can't figure out what's outside and what's inside. Are there people inside? It's impossible to tell. And then I have limited space, right, so I have to tighten up the line to get it to fit. You can link a bunch of sentences together to make more space, but for my purposes, that's a cheat. It ruins the line of the joke. So I have to fit it into the constraint of the space allowed, like a haiku. I figure out that puzzle, that takes me a couple of minutes, and then I turn my attention back to work, and the other part of my mind, my work mind, has figured out how to solve my real problem while I wasn't looking."

"Wow," she said. "My mind doesn't work like that."

"Don't sell yourself short, cupcake," I said. "You're on the faculty of a major medical school. I'm just entertaining myself with nonsense online."

"Most of us don't have that kind of creativity," Annie said. "We need it from you."

> They're razing Crooked Path's Möbius strip mall today. Delicate job. The place has no exits. We haven't been sure who's inside. Or outside.

Duchess:
    May I ask you something extremely personal — about me, not about you? — B

Sure. — DG

I know I'm not a horrible person; that's not the issue. I'm a highly flawed person who occasionally does the wrong things and is capable of hurting people. And has hurt people. I seem, Your Grace, to be having a bit of a panic attack, and I fear I've just overstepped the bounds in this communication, or at least not known when to shut up. — B

Sweets, I am in a store but I'll respond. You're 100% normal and like the rest of us. Not to worry in the least. — DG

You truly cannot imagine what a soul-saver you have been, with just that brief comment. I so appreciate your being there for me. Plus, I like to think of you shopping in your ruff. Thank you for being such a good friend. — B

You know I couldn't do without you. — DG

And the same. — B

Night night, dearest. — DG

Night night, Your Grace. x B

20

Writing isn't hard. Worming my way into your heart one step at a time is hard. But it's holy work, and I bought a boat with the overtime.

M Y SON WAS named for my father, and my father had been named for his uncle, my grandmother's youngest brother. When my grandma was fourteen years old, she was orphaned by her mother's death; her father had died two years earlier. This was 1905. She had two older brothers who were old enough to go off and take care of themselves, but as she was the oldest girl, it fell to her to make sure the younger children were taken care of. In our tradition, a girl is a gift to the family; it's her job to see that everyone's all right. My grandmother went to the parish priest for help, and he arranged to place the young ones in church-run orphanages. She was too old, at fourteen, to take up a bed, so she went out to work. All her life, she remained devoted to the church for saving her younger sisters and brother, for keeping them close by so that she could visit. Keeping the family together was paramount. The youngest brother, who had no memory of his parents, spent ten years in the boys' home before my grandma was in a stable enough position to bust him out. His perspective was completely different from hers. His son told me, years after his death, that he'd privately spoken bitterly about his years in the "home," but I don't think he ever so much as hinted of this to my grandmother. Certainly she believed that the diocesan orphanages had been a gift from God for her family and, anyway, what choice did she have? It was that or starve. Choices are a luxury. We forget that sometimes, don't we? Not everybody gets to have choices.

> If you have the education, wits, and leisure time to pursue your own interests, you have it better than 99% of the people who ever lived.

Having created Duchess as a fictional character who would talk to anyone meant that she did, in fact, have to talk to anyone. She answered every comment people made, and I had a couple of rules: I pushed myself to use every opportunity to respond as a chance to create an inevitable surprise for the reader: "inevitable" in the sense that once you saw it, there was no other response that would have been superior, and a "surprise" in that people couldn't guess what she would say next. I tried to build in surprises around every corner.

Less a rule than a habit, Duchess used pet names for people: rascal, rascalino, sweets, sweetness, love of my life, pumpkin, poodle. She gets that from me. It's handy if I see people and start talking to them before I can recall their names. Plus, you will perhaps agree with me that there are really only about five different names in the world. Put a couple of consonants and vowels together, that's it, that's every name. I can't be expected to remember which random combination of consonants and vowels matches which unique and inherently divine everlasting soul.

I noticed a few years ago that if you consistently call everyone by pet names, no individual person will take offense that you don't call up their name in particular.

Do I walk into work meetings with serious, important people and call them "rascal" and "favorite"? I wish I could tell you no.

("I think I'm developing face blindness," I said to Chuck once.

"You don't have face blindness. You're just not paying attention," he said.)

I'm going to admit this to you privately and only once: it's possible there was some truth to that.

> I have 12 minutes. Ask me anything. Okay, not anything —
> I know you people have no boundaries — ask me
> something not wildly inappropriate.

What's your favorite food to prepare for yourself when you're alone? — JRL

> Coffee. I look forward to it hours in advance, and I sing it a
> little love song when we're together.

What part of marriage did you find happiest, your grace? Before, during, or after the funeral? — K

> I loved being married.

I hope I will. — K

> You will, sweetheart.

How's Hacienda these days? — D

> Sweet Hacienda! You're so kind to ask. She's flourishing.
> She just got the lead in the prison production of OLIVER!

Best advice for dealing with the hardships of life? — E

> Hmmm. I do like to give advice about dealing with
> hardships. Can you specify a particular genre?

How to handle disappointment and the crushing weight of a
broken world? — E

> The world is broken, but you are not broken. Things may
> not be okay, but you're okay, and you will be. I promise.

Thank you, your grace. You are a wonderfully kind soul, even if you
are fictional. — E

> My love is real. I had it tested.

Your love must be real, because it made me cry several real
tears right there in my office cubicle. Thank you, thank you,
thank you. — E

What do you look like? — LP

> Like the hand of God is at work in the world.

Damn, it's past 12 minutes, but if you will . . . how did you meet
Lyle Lovett and April Kimble? — LE

> The angels and saints moved heaven and earth, and
> here we are.

Should an honest admission of guilt be enough to begin
redemption? — O

It's a start, if the admission includes a spirit of contrition: I fully acknowledge and regret the suffering I've caused.

Thank you, your grace. — O

What occupies you during the golden hour of the day? — S

My life's work occupies my mind most of the time.

What if you wake up one day and you're real and we're fictional? Then what? — R

Every day of my life I am real and you are fictional. You only exist for me inside my mind. Isn't that fiction?

21

Maybe every truck on the road is filled with eels. We have no way of knowing. It would certainly explain why we never see eels roaming free.

ONE DAY, DUCHESS wrote that the gates of Crooked Path are guarded by tiny winged bartenders. I think she said bartenders; I don't quite remember.

Lyle was online at that moment and texted me to say Duchess was being especially funny that day, and I texted back to tell him what she'd wanted to say, which was that the gates of Crooked Path are guarded by tiny winged Galveston lesbians. (I'd held her back out of my fear that she's sometimes too much, and someone might be hurt by her nonsensical utterings. I wouldn't want anyone to think I was making fun of lesbians. Why would there be winged Galveston lesbians guarding the gates of a small town in New York? I don't know. I don't question her.)

As soon as he saw my text — *tiny winged Galveston lesbians* — he called, and as I saw his name come up on my phone I answered, and didn't say hello but just laughed and laughed, and he laughed, and it went on that way for some time.

> I'm thinking of a little Etsy shop selling a beautiful boxed set of imaginary friends.

I have some lesbian friends now. I didn't always. I've seemed to draw male friends toward me throughout my life, gay and straight; men have always liked me. I'm comfortable with men. (I know, I know. I get it. The family of origin.) I've looked, over the years, to try to find myself friends and role models and heroes who are women, and when I was younger, yes: I tried to find myself mothers.

But most lesbians, for some reason, haven't ever seemed to care for me. I asked Lorraine, my dear friend who spent most of her youth as a radical lesbian separatist, why she thought this was.

"My theory is that lesbians are put off by my powerful hetero energy," I told her. "Maybe they find it overwhelming, you know what I mean? My raw sexuality. What do you think?"

Lorraine smiled for a second before she burst out laughing at me and shook her head kindly. She patted my arm, chuckling.

"Yeah, no," she said. "No, that's really not it."

So I don't know why lesbians haven't always liked me in real life, but everybody likes Duchess, and she has a fairly strong lesbian following. Why is this, when she is me? If the people who love Duchess met me in real life, would they recognize me?

People often ask me how a fictional being made of spun sugar and justice can overcome life-threatening paper cuts. Simple: It's magic.

Duchess:

My ongoing Duchess fantasy is for you to come to one of my shows where her followers will be. I know I've mentioned this to you before, but I can't shake the image of your standing in the middle of them like Jesus after the resurrection. I wonder how many of them would see her in you. — Lyle

Ha! They wouldn't see me. Isn't there a Bible story in which Jesus appears and the faithful don't recognize him? — DG

That Bible story is one of Jesus's greatest hits! The disciples finally recognized him near the end. Thomas, doubting Thomas, has to touch his hands and feet. I imagine Duchess's followers wanting to do that. — Lyle

Hang on. I can do something with this. — DG

> In today's mailbag: "Duchess, if we faithful saw you in person, would we know you?" Doubt it. Unless you touched my hands and feet. Perverts.

There you are, Lyle. — DG

Perfect! — Lyle

22

Hacienda and I are considering starting a mother-daughter advice column. The usual stuff: beauty tips, criminal defense strategies, poison.

*H*ACIENDA, DUCHESS'S ONLY child, is currently serving a life sentence in a Mexican prison for her crimes against humanity, the details of which Duchess never quite explains.

There are two reasons I have Hacienda in a Mexican prison and why she's never, ever getting out. Maybe three reasons.

Hacienda exists because I knew Duchess had to be a mother. It's important that she not only be a mother, and one who likes to give motherly advice, but a mother whose child is separated from her. It gives her depth she wouldn't have otherwise. If she weren't a mother, she'd be the eternal party girl always sitting at the end of the bar cracking wise, which is fine as far as it goes, but Dorothy Parker did it earlier and better and will never be surpassed.

Hacienda has to remain offstage because Duchess won't share any good lines. I tucked Hacienda away in prison, where she can be safely discussed and referenced but she can't distract, and regular readers understand she's part of the family but doesn't show up and take center stage.

And Duchess has to have wounds that are raw. It's the only thing that explains the sadness that seeps in through the cracks when I'm not looking. Readers can see my scars even when I don't think they're showing.

Missing Hacienda is a shorthand for all the losses Duchess has endured but never enumerated.

I also thought it would be fun to play with a concept that intrigues me: the mother — sometimes it's a father, but I see it more often in mothers — insistent on championing an irredeemable child. You must have known a mother like Duchess at some point. You see them around: at the market, in the Bible, in Greek mythology. They have a kid, either grown or still in childhood, and this kid has no redeeming qualities whatsoever. He's malevolent and badly behaved; he doesn't try to be pleasant. He's not charming, not funny, not kind or smart or big-hearted or talented, not curious about the world, not a good sport, not fun. And yet the mother, the father, will insist on loud adoration.

So Duchess will say, in the same breath, that she's so devoted to her child that she'll make the special effort of a trip to Mexico just to oppose Hacienda's parole again; that Hacienda is her adored child, her beloved, her darling, and let's all pray to God that Hacienda never sees the light of day. Duchess boasts that her daughter took first place in the prison embezzlement games, that she's excelling in her rappelling, tunneling, and archery classes, and that in *Women's Prison Weekly,* Frank Rich called Hacienda Goldblatt "the natural successor to Brian Dennehy" in the prison's production of *The Iceman*

Cometh. I try to make it clear that it's not being in prison itself that's funny in any way, but Duchess's relationship with Hacienda, I hope, is. Likewise, I make it clear that Hacienda's prison is a fantasy prison, with healing yoga retreats and cocktails by the pool.

The prison is in Mexico only because if it were in the US, Duchess would be expected to visit more often, and I can't remember to send her off visiting Hacienda all the time. I've got stuff to do.

> Good night, loons and nutjobs. Good night, dumplings.
> Good night, Las Vegas Duchess Goldblatt impersonators.

Your grace: Discarded book title of the day: SOME QUEEN'S ENGLISH. — Benjamin

Oh, please! Please! I ask for so little in life. — DG

Should I be so fortunate as to have media when the book is published — or ever to tour — you can be damn sure I'll make this joke about a thousand times. — B

Your name came up today on the phone with Lyle. — DG

Oh how lovely. — B

He said, "Benjamin is a world-class mind. How amazing he is. If I could, I would call him every day with usage questions." And I said, "Benjamin is a real fan of yours! He has a fantasy that one day you'll stop by as a surprise and you'll have lunch." And Lyle said, "I should!" I thought you'd get a kick out of that. — DG

This is making me well up a bit. I've had a bad few days. This makes me feel worthwhile. It's like you knew. — B

I felt it just now, as a matter of fact. — DG

Thank you for being such a good friend. — B

> Stand straight, grab your toes, and fling yourself skywards. Oscillate. I believe in you weirdos. Let's make it a beautiful day.

Your grace, I turned in the second draft of the manuscript today. For the first time since I commenced this project, I am able to say the book is complete. Not finished, to be sure, but I didn't, sending it in, have to say, "There are still some holes to fill in." I think I might cry. Hello. — B

I wasn't prepared for the joy, Benjamin. The book! The book! Can we consider it fiction so you can win the Goldblatt Prize? — DG

Sure! — B

Will you get the cover as a piece of art and have it framed? Will I get to meet Mother Dreyer at a launch party? I will come to life for you, you know. I've told you that. — DG

I think I might like to frame the entire jacket once it's finished. (And yes, indeed!) I can't/can believe this is really happening. — B

Believe it. A dream is coming true. — DG

Your grace, of course, is already included in the acknowl-
edgments. Her own paragraph, even. I've been discour-
aged from putting her paragraph in a box, but one can't
have everything. — B

She's asking why a box and not a gold frame. — DG

I'm only getting one color. — B

She thinks her page can be full-color glossy. — DG

Joking apart, it's beginning to seem as if Random House
is beginning to think that something can be made of my
book, which means that the great machine may rev up on
its and my behalf. Which would be delightful. — B

Of course it will. It's going to be huge. — DG

I mean I'm grateful to be published, and the first print-
ing is apt to be at least 20,000 copies, which these days
(NOTHING is selling right now) is perfectly respect-
able, but it would be nice if it really took off. — B

It will. I have a good feeling. — DG

Sweetest of dreams. More tomorrow. X Benjamin

> What happens to you people when I fall asleep? Do you
> cease to exist altogether or do you sit quietly and wait for
> me to come back?

It was true, by the way, that I was doing some of my best work
during this time. I speak now of regular work, which is to say

my real-life job. Duchess doesn't have a job — being eighty-one and a best-selling author and also, for reasons she hasn't otherwise explained, comfortably well-off. Frankly, it's easier for me if she doesn't work. It streamlines the plot, which comes in handy as I can't always remember what she's said from one day to the next. It keeps her schedule open, and it saves me from introducing other characters, like any pain-in-the-ass colleagues. If you read Duchess regularly, you could believe she's an elderly woman of leisure. She's making conversation with strangers in New Zealand at two in the morning.

But I, on the other hand, have to work every day, and when I'm not working, I'm thinking about work. An easy way to explain what I do is that I distill the complex findings of researchers in different areas into smaller, more usable pieces for practical use by corporations willing to pay for it. I mostly work on a laptop in my extra bedroom, and as long as I get a ton of work done, no one cares what time of day or night I do it. Time expands and contracts on its own when the clock never registers quitting time. Very often I don't know what day it is, particularly if my kiddo isn't home with me. I forget to eat. I forget to stop. Once or twice a month I make a special guest appearance in our headquarters, but I consider those days lost to productivity. I get very distracted by people, so all I do is prance around and visit with everyone. Bob Hope on a USO tour of our office, if you will. Right now I have, I think, twenty-seven active projects at different stages of development, and I can see them all in my head at once. Each project, every conversation I have, every piece of the work is all written on a piece of paper in my head, and I'm moving the lines around all the time.

Conversations I overhear get noted in the margins as little scribbles, unless they're more interesting to me than the conversation I'm in, in which case I slide the lines of my own conversation to the left and move my gaze to the conversation I'm eavesdropping on so I can pay better attention to it. This sometimes means I have to ask the people I'm speaking with to be quiet and stop talking so I can eavesdrop more effectively.

I can see individual sentences, those that I've written and those I'm going to write, but also paragraphs and subsections and the layout and graphic components, and the relationships of the people who are connected to each project, their names as text but also their spoken words as text, alongside the messages they've sent me and calendars of deadlines: all those parts are on the page in my mind, shifting as needed, while my phone is next to me, and if I notice my phone there, I might pick it up out of habit and be Duchess for a minute:

> When people say they're going to "make time for you,"
> it's instant time from a mix. Nobody bothers creating new
> time from scratch anymore.

And then I click the phone off and go back to work, to my happy place: my projects and the pieces of paper in my head.

Our fiscal year ended maybe a month ago.

Chuck called me in to his office and said, "The numbers are all in. You're making some of us look bad again."

"You want me to slow down?" I said. "I guess I could. I could take more naps. I do get tired a lot."

"No, but I can't explain how you're taking on so many projects and finishing them," Chuck said. "This one" — he pointed to a line item on a spreadsheet — "you billed sixty-seven hours, start to finish. All of our metrics say it should have taken you four hundred hours. I'm going to have to tell the board you've got some kind of weird black magic going on that can't be replicated."

"Maybe I'm a miracle and the universe is sending you a sign that you should give me a raise," I said.

He snorted. "Bratface."

"Ingrate."

"Diva!" But he was smiling. "This is the version of you I've been waiting for. You're rocking it. I knew you had it in you to come back."

"Okay," I said. "All right, very good. Let me get back to my work, rascal."

Outperforming other people is of no interest to me. It certainly doesn't motivate me. If anything, it makes me feel a little guilty. I was raised not to show off, not to be proud, not to draw attention to myself. I don't like people looking at me or standing too close. Compliments make me uncomfortable. My greatest childhood dream was to be an author whom everyone would read but no one would look at directly, but I couldn't figure out a way to write books without people knowing my name. (A word in your ear: I think I might have finally figured out a tiny loophole just big enough for me to slip through.)

My other childhood dream was to grow old on a deserted island by myself; I thought it would be lovely to be an old man with a long white beard sitting in flowing robes underneath a palm tree on a patch of sandy island, just looking out at the ocean forever. I haven't quite found a way to make that dream come true yet.

Duchess likes to be looked at, to be praised and admired; in fact, she insists on it. She butts into conversations; she turns people's attention to herself.

> I look so beautiful today. It's really hard for me to concentrate. I don't know how any of you manage to get your work done with me around.

Me: no. I don't like being seen. I'd always rather be eavesdropping, watching people, standing at the back of the room with avenues of egress readily available just in case I need to split. I'm not competitive, which I used to flatter myself was a sign of maturity, but I realized a few years ago it could also be arrogance. I just don't care enough about what other people are doing to compete with them. I see myself not in competition with anybody but in partnership with the page itself. It's the beauty of the work that interests me, even if, like Duchess Goldblatt, like a Tibetan monk's sand painting, it's ephemeral. I will make it as perfect as I can while I work on it, and it will not hurt my heart when the wind sweeps it all away.

> Look at me, child. Have you ever seen any greater testimony to the glory of God's handiwork than the face of Duchess Goldblatt?

Duchess's relentless insistence on her own physical beauty is both a running joke and a call to others to see and acknowledge their own gifts. When we rely on self-deprecating humor, we're trying to neutralize criticism preemptively, and there are echoes of ancient superstitions. I will deny my own gifts so that the gods don't punish me and take them away.

Duchess goes the other direction. Her old heart is broken and in tatters, but the world is beautiful and she loves it. She makes herself as large as possible. She reminds people that they're better than they give themselves credit for, that their creative efforts matter, that they have a responsibility to extend themselves on the side of righteousness and do their best work. It's part of the reason that she holds herself up as an example of physical beauty. If Duchess Goldblatt announces herself as beautiful, how can you not also acknowledge your own beauty?

I needed a word today and it eluded me for three hours. Finally, I treed it and put a canned ham outside. It'll come down when it's ready.

Tell me: if there were a contest between who/what I would like more, You or Your Book, which would win? — PJ

The book, friend. — DG

Interesting. I think it might be a tie. But who knows? Not me on either front. Thank you for calling me your friend. — PJ

Of course you're my friend. — DG

That's nice. I don't want to miss out on you. — PJ

You are not missing out on me. This is literally all there is. I talk to you more than anyone. — DG

I know. I believe you. I'd like to think I'd know your voice or recognize your face in a crowd. I'm old-fashioned. — PJ

Lyle and I have discussed it and we think you would not know me unless you touched my hands and feet. — DG

That is fascinating. I mean, I'll do whatever. I'll try really hard not to keep bugging you for more forms of contact. — PJ

What is it that you think would be different if you saw me prancing down the street? — DG

I don't know. It feels natural to wish for that. When I care about people, I usually try to see them and talk to them. It's basic to my nature. — PJ

I see. You want to pat my head, as it were. — DG

Yes. And develop fondnesses. I am ready to see you. — PJ

Why haven't you mentioned this before? — DG

I believe it was implied. — PJ

Let me check the transcripts. — DG

> Sometimes it's hard for me to fall asleep at night because I know I'll miss myself when I'm gone.

My father used to try to tell me to never say anything about anyone that I wouldn't want them to overhear.

"It will make you boring in conversation sometimes," he said. "Maybe you know something private about someone that's embarrassing and you could say it at a party, make everybody laugh. You'll have to hold yourself back from doing it. Give up the fun of getting that laughter for yourself. But if you believe that you're called to never cause pain to another human being, it won't be a hard choice."

I've had a very hard time learning that lesson. I'm still trying to learn it. The mean joke is always right there at my fingertips. It's effortless. Any asshole can make a mean joke. It's harder work to reach out further for the joke that's funny and can't hurt anybody.

I came to realize, over time, that a dig made at a famous person for ordinary human failings, no matter how far removed they are from the conversation, carries with it an implied criticism of the reader. To make fun of anyone diminishes my reader. It diminishes me.

So when a celebrated artist is arrested on a DUI or an actor says something stupid: these are easy marks. I could get laughs. But why? There's no writing challenge in it, and there's no magic, either. Gertrude Stein was talking about Oakland, California, when she said, "There's no there there," but she could have just as easily been talking about social media. I try to find the there that's hidden there, or to plant some there there and watch it grow.

> No, frankly, I don't agree that I'm setting an impossible beauty standard. You could go put on a nicer ruff and ensaucen your sly gaze.

I went away for a few days to visit some of my dear ones. I've told you I have a few people in other states to whom Duchess refers, collectively, as her "Man on the Outside," meaning that they're willing to receive packages for her and give them to me. This time, her Man on the Outside had collected a few shipments in his front hall closet: CDs and a band T-shirt from Dean Sabatino, aka "Dean Clean," the drummer from the punk band the Dead Milkmen; Jason Fagone's nonfiction book *The Woman Who Smashed Codes;* Nick Arvin's novel *Mad Boy;* candy and socks and the novel *Skin Deep,* from Liz Nugent in Ireland; a coffee mug with Duchess's picture on it.

"Why are people sending you all this stuff?" my Man on the Outside asked me, handing me the packages.

"They love Duchess," I said.

"What do you mean, they love her? They don't even know you," he said.

"It's a distant love and affection for the person you think

you know. Same way you might love any celebrity," I said. "Tiger Woods, for example."

"I could say I admired his game. I certainly wouldn't say I ever *loved* him," he said.

"Well, that was just the first random famous name I thought of. Okay then, say Steph Curry."

"I don't like the Warriors."

"What warriors?"

"You just said Steph Curry from the Golden State Warriors."

"That was just an example. I was trying to find a cultural reference we both know."

"But you don't know it. You don't even know what team he's on."

"I know his wife is the chef Ayesha Curry. She's adorable."

"Adorable!" chimed in the other Man on the Outside, who although technically not a man does meet the critical Man on the Outside job criteria of being located out of state and harboring a cheerful willingness to forward Duchess's mail.

"You know the other one I love is Giada," added Man on the Outside #2. "And who's that young one? He's got a cookbook."

"The one with the hair? Oh, no," I said. "No, I know the one you mean. Everything's fresh. Not the naked guy. The other one. I can't think of his name right now."

"I'll tell you who I love, and that's Ina Garten," Man on the Outside #2 said.

"See, there's my point: you can love a celebrity without ever knowing them personally," I said.

"You're not a celebrity," my Man on the Outside reminded me.

"No," I agreed. "Don't tell Duchess."

I'm teaching a group of youngsters to use humor to make friends. I'll pull out the old razzle-dazzle! That's how I passed the California bar.

The CEO of my company saw me in the office one day and flagged me down.

"How's your new project coming along?" he asked.

I knew why he was asking. I'd been assigned to a project with an external partner to whom he'd made a lot of promises. It was high profile, highly visible to the board, very important to the organization for a number of strategic reasons. He was anxious that everything should go well.

Normally, I'd be a little nervous to be called out that way. I would have stammered something simple, something small and defensive: "It's fine. Everything's fine."

But inside my heart, I stood back a minute and nudged the door open a crack to let her out. Duchess came flouncing through the door, as expected, and pushed me aside. She grabbed the mic.

"Be at peace about the project," I found myself saying to the CEO, loud enough for everyone around us to hear. "The partner falls ever more deeply in love with me as we live and flourish."

He burst out in a surprised laugh. He's not generally a big laugher. A few people nearby lifted their heads to listen to us.

"Why do you question it?" I asked him. "What have you heard?"

"Certainly nothing negative," he said. "I talked to her this morning. She said it's going very well."

"READ BETWEEN THE LINES, SON," I said. "She can't be any more clear about her love for me," and he laughed harder.

"Good," he said, with a nod, and kept walking. "That's what I like to hear." I turned around and saw Chuck leaning in a doorway behind me, grinning. "There you are," he said. "I knew you were in there somewhere."

> To be fair, they'll let anybody be a poet laureate these days. All you need is 50 cents, four Cheerios box tops, and a drawing of a turtle.

Duchess: I remember, before we started conversing, that I said out loud to someone, "I'm probably never going to tell Duchess much of anything privately. She could be ANYONE. I have no way of knowing who I'm talking to." I was all resolute and rigid and sure of myself and my boundaries. And then I talked to you anyway. — PJ

Interesting. My memory is a little different. I seem to recall you've been obsessed from the beginning. Weren't you the one who made about 500 coffee mugs with Duchess's face? Didn't you take a laminated picture of Duchess all around Paris with you? — DG

True. I remember following you and I thought you were a lot of fun. I can't remember when or how or why you followed me back. — PJ

Oh, I remember why. I was in the market for an emotionally healthy and functional friend. You edged out a number of other candidates. — DG

We didn't really start conversing frequently until I started winding down on social media. I was being more private, and you understood that, and that felt really nice to me. It was a relief and felt like a grace. — PJ

You gave me good advice. You said you liked to let other people solve their problems themselves. — DG

It's true. When I was the boss at my old job, people would approach me with bullshit problems and I would stare at them hard and say, "How would you solve this problem if I didn't exist?" — PJ

That's really good. I'm stealing that. — DG

I'm going to say something sappy and then we'll move on as if I never said it. Please be careful when you're driving. I care about you. I prefer you safe and sound and alive. I should probably look for you in New Jersey. — PJ

Yes, poodle. Look for me first in your heart. — DG

> The American Psychiatric Association is pushing hard to get a blurb from me for the DSM-6.

DG: I just saw what you wrote. Brilliant, as always. — Lyle

Lyle: I thought of something funnier, but I was afraid it might be too mean. It hurts my heart when I can't say the very funniest thing I think of, because I'm vain enough to want to show off, but one of DG's principles is that she doesn't poke fun "at" anyone. — DG

That's a great rule of life, a great lesson for us all. Duchess is ever mindful. It's her unconditional acceptance that makes her so beloved. You are invisible glue made of good will. — Lyle

Thank you. I'll tell you my theory on poking fun. I ran this by a group of Cub Scouts when I taught them a lesson on using humor to make friends, and it resonated with the children, so I think there's a fundamental truth in it. If I make a joke at another person's expense, even a gentle joke, even if the person is beyond the reach of my voice and will never know it or be hurt by it: it diminishes my listener to hear it; it diminishes me to tell it. The better joke is always going to be the one that doesn't hurt anybody. This is the habit of mind I work at. — DG

I couldn't agree more. I also try to maintain that kind of respect for other living creatures. You're exactly right, it regards someone as less than human — less than a living, breathing being with feelings. I bet it was funny. But I get it. It's better, I agree, to take the right path, not just the easy path. It's really great work. You really touch people. — Lyle

Thank you, Lyle. That means the world to me. — DG

As you do to me, your grace. — Lyle

Good night, world, you old loon. I love you.

23

I found a box of old hours at the back of the fridge. I don't
even know how long it had been there. Summer hours.
Smelled like roses.

*T*HERE IS ANOTHER person out there in the world somewhere, a mother, who loves Duchess deeply. She and
Duchess have been corresponding for years, one tiny note at
a time, another tiny note at a time, like two prisoners tapping
out messages to each other on the walls of their cells. We'd become close somehow, through these different truncated ver-
sions of ourselves. I'd become attached to her through her
writing. She'd gotten attached to Duchess, as people do.

We got a chance to be in the same city once, and we met
face to face. When we had a moment together alone, I had to
tell her that I was Duchess. To stand next to her and look her
in the eye and not admit that we'd corresponded privately as
two close friends would have felt like lying.

I leaned over and whispered to her, "I'm Duchess Goldblatt."

"Yes. I thought you were," she said with a nod.

I didn't even ask how she knew. If she didn't need Duchess to remain an imaginary friend, then I didn't need her to, either.

"I've wanted so badly for you to give me a hug and call me honey bunch," she said.

Of course I was thrilled to give her a hug. Of course I was happy to call her honey bunch.

Yesterday her child died, and she came looking for Duchess via a private message online.

Duchess: Please hold me tight. My heart has a giant hole now.

I can feel her grief from across the country. There once was a time when that overwhelming grief in someone else would have panicked me. But because I know what it is to mourn, I can feel that darkness gathering in someone else's heart. It would have been unbearable to me to sit still with it. Once upon a time, I would have run away.

But now I know I can hold her peacefully within my heart and still have room left over. If this is the result of my own sorrow — an enlarged capacity; the ability to contain heartbreak not my own — if this was the deal, then it's acceptable to me. Duchess Goldblatt wasn't the one who taught me that grief would expand the boundaries of my heart, but she was the one who showed me how to share it with other people. This is not the life I wanted — I have mourned with every piece of my old broken heart for the life I always wanted, the happy family I couldn't make out of thin air and good intentions for my kid and me — but this is the life I seem to have been groomed for.

Duchess: I need all the love I can absorb, and more. People keep saying holidays will be difficult and I think, how difficult can it be when everyday life is difficult. Oh, but holidays ARE difficult.

I hope your snow and clouds where you are treat you kindly, Duchess. I wish I could think of one thing that would make you laugh.

May we have a better year coming. Love to you —

"She told me she met you in real life before. She found out who you are," a mutual friend told Duchess in a private message. "She said she found out your real name about a year ago, but she confessed she's forgotten by now what it is. It seemed perfect, somehow: incredibly meaningful to have met you, but then you returned to full Goldblattitude."

"That's perfect," I wrote back. "Nothing remains but Duchess."

Good night, rascals, dreamboats, and hermits.
Good night, crackpots and nutjobs and scoundrels.
Good night, all librarians everywhere.

I need you to get a GoPro camera. — PJ

Why? — DG

I truly want to watch your life. I want to watch people's faces. — PJ

All I really do is work. Sometimes I prance around and say funny things. — DG

You know how to live. I want to be friends with you. — PJ

I am sure that if you meet me you will leave me. — DG

I am sure you are wrong about that. What is it about you
(or me!) that you think would make me leave you? — PJ

It's hard-wired into my brain. Everyone goes, sooner or
later. — DG

It's a life theme. We should change it. — PJ

I went out to lunch with people and I realized, PJ, I realized. — DG

YES? — PJ

I've never had a really satisfying crab cake. I always think
it will be better than it is. — DG

I never get those. I know it's a dirty trick. — PJ

Same with lobster rolls. Plus lobsters are smart. They can
read cartoons. — DG

With an IQ of like 43, right? — PJ

90–150. — DG

I just googled. They're as smart as octopuses. — PJ

They can pass the Connecticut bar. Of course, they usually can't come up with the entrance fees. — DG

There's my Duchess. Before I go, I'm going to tell you
something about trust. It goes like this: It's best if you de-

cide to be true to the relationship rather than being true to the person. Because when the person lets you down (and he/she will!), you'll say to yourself, "All bets are off!" And you'll feel free to break a trust or breach privacy or be disloyal in big or small ways. It's a justification. If you commit to the relationship, you're being faithful to that. Same with friendship. That's what I endeavor to do. — PJ

24

Good night, friends. Try not to fall ever more hopelessly in love with me tonight.

WHEN I GRADUATED from college, I didn't make any plans to attend the ceremonies. I figured they could mail me the diploma later, or not. It didn't matter. My father was dead. I didn't have the heart to go without him.

A week or two beforehand, my favorite professor, Al, pulled me aside.

"I know you're not going to walk at commencement," Al said. "But if you change your mind, just call me. Even at the last minute. I'll have an extra cap and gown for you. I'll take care of everything."

"That's very kind," I said. "But I don't think I have it in me. There's no point in going without my father. It doesn't matter anymore."

"I'm sure your dad would want you to go," he said.

"Yeah."

"Okay," Al said. "I won't push. You think about it."

So I thought about it, and somehow, at the last minute, I decided: Okay, maybe I should go, just for myself. I called Al at home and his wife answered. When I introduced myself, she cheered.

"Let me get him," she said. "He's been hoping you would call."

Al pulled up to my apartment in his silver Volvo. He came out of the car carrying a huge bouquet of flowers for me, along with the promised cap and gown. I think I walked and got my diploma that day; I don't remember. I guess I must have. No one else was there for me, which wasn't a surprise; I'd told my surviving relatives not to come, and I hadn't ever made a friend while I was in college, understandably. During those years I was in school full-time, I had a scholarship plus a job to maintain, and my father was failing badly. He'd needed daily hands-on care.

Al was my friend, but he was one of the most beloved professors on campus. He was everybody's friend. After the ceremony, Al dodged all the other students who wanted hugs and photos with him, and we legged it back to the Volvo. He drove us to a nearby park, where he pulled out a six-pack of beer.

"Let's go for a walk and sit up on that hill over there," he said. "And you can tell me all about your dad."

It was so kind, so unexpected. He ditched everyone else on graduation day to spend it with me. It sounds now, as I tell the story so many years later, as if we were close. We weren't. He hardly knew me. He would have done the same for any graduating senior. If you've ever wondered what the right thing is to say to someone who's grieving a death, I think this is it: *Tell me all about your dear one.*

Sometimes I think of something so funny that I break out laughing by myself, and it's then that I know you're with me.

Dear Duchess:

As I read your quote from Frank Delaney, "When you have no one to put their arms around you, you must put your arms around yourself," it surprised me. Knowing you and knowing how you embrace your followers, how you help them, I imagined his words of advice to be "You must put your arms around others."

Because that's what you do and that's why Duchess is important. If being Duchess began as a selfish act, then it's a perfect win-win. If by being Duchess for yourself you're able to help people, give them a voice, and make them feel cared about, you've struck the perfect balance in life.

When God created the world, I don't believe it was in the spirit of altruism. I think it had to be more in the spirit of "I wonder what would happen if I ... hmmm, that might be fun."

Can a writer's in-person persona affect a reader's interest in the writer's work? I think it can. That's something I think about a lot regarding my songs and their presentation in live performance. Does the audience think of me as a character in my songs? How important is that perception to their interest? I think it's all mixed together.

With love from the bus, somewhere in Greensboro, NC,

Lyle

Lyle,

I think you can get attached to the artist's persona. I think the fans see you as a character in your songs but not as a fixed character, if you will. So "Creeps Like Me," we know that you're not the creep; but we see you, your humor and wit, coming through that voice. And the body of work together along with your demeanor onstage and graciousness and kindness, your generosity with the other musicians — the whole package, yes, I think it's all revealing, all important.

xo — DG

Thanks for your insights as always.

I'm excited about your book. The world needs it. I need it.

Your friend,
Lyle

Close your eyes and visualize the best possible outcome. When it's not looking, grasp it by the neck and fling it into reality.

The night before Benjamin Dreyer's book, *Dreyer's English,* was making its formal publishing debut, he hosted a party on Forty-Second Street in New York and invited Duchess. It was a small affair for his close friends and family, and, as she had promised him years earlier, Duchess Goldblatt came to life for it.

I stood at the back of the room and waited for him to notice me, and when he made no motion toward me through the crowd or even glanced my way, I finally sidled up alongside him, shoulder to shoulder. I didn't look at him, but I gave a surreptitious little tug on his sleeve at the elbow.

"Benjamin," I murmured under my breath. "It's me."

"I know it's you."

I gestured to the long scarf I had wound several times

around my neck. "I wore a ruff so you'd know me," I said. He started to laugh and well up with tears at the same time. He pulled me into a private room away from the party.

When we were alone, he said, "You're everything I ever hoped you would be and more."

"More? What do you mean *more?*"

"Because you're real," he said. "You're good and you're true and you're here. And you're real."

> Good morning, sentient chunks of goodness. We meet
> again for another spin on the old axis. Let's see what we
> can do with this one.

After the party, I had one more stop to make before leaving New York. I made my way over to a tiny Italian restaurant in Hell's Kitchen and stumbled through the bar crowd to a little table in back where my old friend James was waiting. I slid a confidentiality agreement across the table to him.

James rolled his eyes at me. "How long have we been friends?"

"Come on. Just sign it. Then I can tell you my happy news."

"Fine." He signed, and added, "This better be good."

"I sold the book."

"That's so exciting!" James cried, and grabbed both my hands in his for a squeeze. He lifted his glass of wine to toast and then he sighed. "Goddamnit. You know Duchess Goldblatt was my drag queen name."

"I know. But to be fair, you weren't using it."

"No," he agreed. "I was never going to use it. And you've done the name proud."

Hello, lemon-lime sourballs. It's Transitory Saturday, when we remember that nothing is good forever, and nothing is bad forever.

"So now Benjamin knows your name!" Lyle said on the phone a few days later.

"You know, come to think of it, I don't think I told him my name."

"What do you mean you didn't tell him? How do you meet someone and not tell him your name?"

"It didn't come up."

"You went all the way to New York to his party to meet him and you didn't think to tell him your name?"

"He didn't ask."

"So what did he call you?"

"I'm not sure. We fell into a joyous embrace and he hugged me and kissed me and we cried. I think he called me your grace."

"If that isn't the damnedest thing I ever heard," Lyle said.

25

When I find myself in need of great beauty, I close my eyes and listen, and it slips in through the side door.

*D*O YOU THINK if your brother was alive today, they could help him now?" my cousin Warren asked me once.

I knew what he meant. I'd wondered it myself. The medications and treatments they have today are far superior to what was available back then, even at the best hospitals. And they know so much more about the brain and biochemistry and addiction than they knew then.

"Maybe?" I said. "If they'd gotten to him early enough? I don't even know if they ever even got a diagnosis for him. I'm not sure he ever stayed long enough in a hospital or cooperated enough with the doctors to get one. Or if they did give him a diagnosis, nobody ever told me what it was. He was so difficult to deal with. He wouldn't accept help; he didn't want to get better. As long as I knew him, all he ever wanted was to die."

"Even when he was a kid?"

"I didn't know him when he was a kid. In my earliest memories of him, I would have been five or six, so he was fifteen, sixteen; and, yes, he was already suicidal by then, already showing signs of serious mental illness. People noticed, of course, but I don't think anyone around him had a way to understand what they were seeing. My parents tried to get help for him later. They put him in hospitals; people tried to help him. But for someone with his intellect, I don't know how much anyone could have helped him when he didn't want it. He was so much smarter than everybody else."

He blinked. He'd known my brother. "Smarter? Nah. He was a bright kid, sure, but that's all."

That was a genuine shock to my ears. It had been gospel in my childhood home that my brother had been one of the greatest minds of his generation, maybe. Top ten, anyway.

"He was brilliant. A star," I said. "A genius."

"What?" he said. "I don't know where you got that. If anything, you were —"

"Nope," I said. I couldn't hear it. My heart was beating out of my chest. This was close to blasphemy. No one had ever, ever doubted my brother's complete superiority. He was the extraordinary one. I worked harder, I was the one who tried, but he had been given favor.

On the night I was born, there was a pink moon. I'd always been told what that meant: a girl was a gift to the family. I was supposed to take care of him.

> I spilled a bag of ellipses all over the floor. Now I don't know where anything begins or ends.

26

It's such a beautiful night. I think I'll catch up on reading your diaries. I'll use track changes so you can see where you went wrong.

I'VE READ YOUR book," said my aunt. "Seven times. I was just about to start it for the eighth time and I thought I'd call instead."

"Oh?"

"Every time I read it, Duchess teaches me something new."

We laughed. Oh, that Duchess!

"The family parts were hard for me to read, of course," she said.

"Yes, I'm sorry. I know it's painful."

"It's very painful for me. I can only imagine how painful it was for you. The parts with your brother — I guess I didn't realize how bad it was. Looking back, I don't know how I didn't see it. Why didn't I see it? I'm so angry at myself for not helping you more in your growing-up years. When you checked him out of the hospital by yourself: I remember that. Why did we let you do that alone? I should have helped more."

"No, remember how protective my parents were of him. They didn't want anybody to know. They would never have let you come near."

"I still can't help thinking I should have seen it. And the parts with your dad." She paused. "I know how you loved him. We all loved him. He was a wonderful person."

"Yeah."

"But your father was not perfect. He had his flaws just like anybody else."

"I know."

She started to say something and then stopped herself and started over. "Duchess is so special. But she's you. It's your voice. It's your ideas and your humor. She's not your father. Just like my children are not me. You give him all the credit for Duchess, and I know he was a wonderful person — but, honey, she's you."

"Yeah," I said.

We know.

> I don't mind an unreliable narrator, as long as she's punctual.

"Some of your followers came to our show last night," Lyle told me on the phone, rattling off a list of names. "April and I have met so many great people through you. I can't believe the number of people we've met because of you. You are like a litmus test, you know. I know if people are followers of yours they're going to be nice, they're going to be so kind and fun and smart. That's your book, you know: the community you've created through Duchess."

"Is it?"

"I think so. And how's the book coming?" he asked.

"Well, a few people have read it now."

"What did they say?"

"People have read it so deeply, Lyle. What a gift to have your work read so carefully! I had no idea. They had a few suggestions for how I might improve it, and I thought —"

"No. No."

"I thought they made some valid points —"

"No. You don't need to change a thing. You're Duchess Goldblatt. You know better than anybody what you should write."

"A couple of people have asked if I could find a way to give it a happier ending," I said.

"A happy ending? They missed the whole point. Well, I'll tell you what: see if you can give Duchess some sex scenes. That ought to do it."

I laughed. She'd love that. "I'm trying to make myself a happy ending in real life, and then I can put a happy ending in the book," I said. "Efforts have been made."

"I know your book is perfect."

"I appreciate that, Lyle, I do. But, to be fair," I had to add, "you haven't read it yet."

"I don't need to read it. I know it's perfect."

"I'm grateful for your enthusiasm, Lyle," I said.

"Just finish the book," Lyle said. "The world needs you to."

"You're a real friend, you know that?" I said. "I haven't always had one before."

"You're one of my only real friends, too," he said. "Everybody else is on the payroll."

I laughed, and he said, no, not really. He was joking. But I knew what he meant. He meant that our friendship was pure, like those that are forged early in childhood. You ever see two little kids running around together? They're only aware of extracting the greatest possible fun out of that moment. That was our friendship.

> I want to drop by your dreams tonight. When you're falling asleep, hold a little empty space for me in your mind.

When the book did sell, I grabbed the phone to tell my friends, and I was shocked to realize how many people there were I wanted to tell: Lyle, Chuck, Jackie, my aunt and uncle, of course, but new friends from work, from the neighborhood and the kid's school, Benjamin Dreyer and PJ, Elizabeth Mc-Cracken, author and editor friends, artists, musicians, friendly nutjobs. I started looking around the world and realized: I have friends again. I've built myself a civilization from the ashes.

I brought my jewelry to the jeweler: what was left, what I hadn't sold off years earlier.

"I want to trade in these two," I said, pushing my wedding ring and anniversary band across the table to him. "Let's put them toward the cost of the new project, but be sure to melt them down. Don't try to resell them as they are. They've got some bad mojo on them."

He lifted his chin, not agreeing or disagreeing. Letting me know he heard.

"And then these stones I want reset in a right-hand cluster ring," I told him, putting all my family pieces in front of him. "A statement ring. I have something to celebrate."

"It'll be gorgeous. But I think you don't want ostentatious," he said.

"No, I'm okay with ostentatious," I said.

He held the largest sapphire. Even without a loupe, he could see there were flaws. "There is some wear on this."

"Of course. It's old. My father gave that sapphire to me when I was twelve."

I showed him a drawing I'd made of a ring with the jewels in an asymmetrical cluster pattern. "Oh, you're thinking really asymmetrical," he said.

I nodded. "Crooked."

"Crooked, okay. So all your stones are white and blue, but coming from these different pieces like they are, your blues aren't perfectly matched. If you extend the palette but stay within the same family, it would make more sense from a color perspective. Maybe add in a couple small sapphires in a lighter blue or light blue-green to pull it together." He pulled out a box of artists' pencils and started choosing blues and greens to sketch with. "I always like it when people make something new out of old jewelry. Why not use what you have to make something beautiful?"

"And I want an inscription that means something to me," I added.

"Of course." He held his pencil and waited.

"Feasting on the carcasses of my enemies."

The old jeweler glanced up at me over his half-glasses. "We're going to need a bigger ring."

> If you don't use autocorrect, it will wither and fall off.
> It will be forgotten by future generations, much like
> autodeface and autoabsolve.

It was Lyle who convinced me that I was inherently worthy, that if I cast my inner light out into the universe, more light would bounce back toward me. And lo! The more I've become Duchess and myself at once, both of us together with one voice, the more that my real tribe has been able to find me. Fancy that.

I wish I had learned all my lessons sooner. I'm old already. I don't know how that happened; I tried so hard to be careful.

I sat down to write a letter to Frank Delaney, to tell him I'm all right now, that my heart is at peace, that I've learned how to put my arms around myself. I've stopped pushing people away, Frank, at least a little. I've learned how to spot a friend when I see a new one in the wild. I've found my voice. Duchess is still in Crooked Path, and Hacienda will always be in a Mexican prison — somehow the two of them are bending time and space to cohost a bake sale fundraiser for the Dorothy Parker Academy for Girls this weekend — but Duchess doesn't respond to everyone anymore. She's receding. I know now I won't lose the sounds passing through sudden rightnesses because it was always just me, singing my own song to keep myself company. I'm okay and my kid will be okay, and this is what the ancestors prayed for.

When I sat down to write to Frank Delaney, I discovered to my great sorrow that he had died a few months earlier following a stroke. I never got the chance to tell him. Instead I'm telling you: my rascals, my loons, my sweethearts.

Long live Duchess Goldblatt.

Acknowledgments

I offer grateful thanks to this book's first readers, including my adored aunt and uncle, whose names are carved on the palms of my hands. Benjamin C. Dreyer provided not only crucial guidance but enthusiastic cheerleading. Howard Mittelmark made critical suggestions that proved essential. There is no greater triumvirate of supporters than Lyle Lovett, Elizabeth McCracken, and Rebecca Makkai: I am rich beyond measure in these brilliant and loving people I am honored to call friends.

Let it be known that Elizabeth McCracken acknowledged me first, but I have loved her always.

This dream would not have come true without the team of superheroes at Houghton Mifflin Harcourt fully behind it with their energy, passion, and expertise: Helen Atsma, Bruce Nichols, Emma Gordon, Hannah Harlow, Lori Glazer, Erin DeWitt, Jenny Xu, Jenny Freilach, Allison Chi, and Pilar Garcia-Brown. Naomi Gibbs, an editor of uncommon grace and power, has been a guiding light.

I remain dazzled by and grateful for the patronage of two

guardian angels: my secret weapon, Lucy Carson of the Friedrich Agency, who has led every charge while shielding my weary old heart; and editor Lauren Wein, who took my hand in darkness and walked me toward the dawn. *Becoming Duchess Goldblatt* exists because of Lucy Carson. If you can clearly see truth and beauty through this kaleidoscope, it's largely because of Lauren Wein.

Sending my fondest love to all the virtual dear ones whose kind friendliness out in the world lit the way to Crooked Path and back again. I'm 100% sure you gave me more than I ever gave you.

A Conversation with the Author

Originally published in the Amazon Book Review

What state of affairs was going on in the world that convinced you a Duchess was sorely needed to *Become* and rescue us?
                                                              — *Kit Ontko*
Duchess Goldblatt: It's lovely that you credit me with bringing Duchess Goldblatt, this fictional character, into being to rescue others or to help the world. I didn't intend anything of the kind. I was only trying to cheer myself up and have a few laughs. It was other people who found something worthwhile in her fictional presence online and decided they wanted to keep reading her.

To whom does Duchess Goldblatt turn for solace in the way we look to Duchess Goldblatt?
                                                              — *Kris Simmons, Chicago*
She looks out and about in the world for little bits and pieces of solace that she can polish up and bring home, and she finds

it everywhere. There's so much in this world that she finds to take delight in. Evil is sort of having a heyday right now — it always has much better PR — but turning the other cheek is nonviolent resistance, it's actively turning away from evil. It's a conscious turning away from the darkness and toward the light. I think that's what Duchess is up to most of the time.

What is the true origin of your cleverness, and how shall we locate it within ourselves?

— *Annette Januzzi Wick, Cincinnati*

There are people who can look in an empty pantry, and where I'd see nothing — half a bag of flour and a can of chickpeas — they see dinner. They can make something wonderful out of whatever they find. It's a skill that comes from long practice and need. I think you're onto something when you say you'll locate the origin within yourself. When I was young, I worked for a while as a waitress, and I said half-jokingly to a much older waitress, "What am I going to do with my life?" And she — she was a Buddhist, a contemplative person — said, "You have to figure out what gifts you have to offer the world." Her gift was kindness, and of course, she was right. It's that looking inward, that deep looking inward, where you find the origin of the raw material you have to work with.

Could you give us your thoughts on the Velveteen Rabbit Principle? (Being loved enough can make us Real?)

— *Audrey Niffenegger, Chicago*

I guess it depends on what "Real" means. And, for that matter, it depends on what being loved "enough" is. A person of faith might say they love God so much that God is Real to them: ever present, ever alive. You and I might agree that you can love a fictional character so much that you keep that character fully alive and present in your mind. So yes, I think your love can make the rabbit Real for *you*. But does the rabbit become Real to herself based on someone else's love? Fleetingly, maybe. If I love myself based on my reflection as seen in other people's eyes that's ultimately a superficial kind of love; it's not unchanging through time. It will fade. For the rabbit to become Real to herself, that love has to spring authentically from a deeper well within. It has to carry the spark of the divine.

How can I become fictional, like you?
— *Kit, Edmonton, Alberta, Canada*
You have to sit very, very still for a long time, alone, until the self recedes and another self emerges from the wreckage. It stings like the dickens. I don't necessarily recommend it.

On the other hand, I'm saying this as myself, a regular living person, and Duchess Goldblatt is a fictional character who lives inside my head, and none of this hurt her one bit. She's thrilled that you're paying attention to her. She's pushing me out of the way and taking another bow.

Exactly how delightful is it to be so beloved?
— *Ellen T, Nebraska*
Duchess Goldblatt is greatly beloved, and I can see that love flourishing before my eyes; I can watch it from behind the curtain, where I'm alone, and enjoy it the way you might enjoy seeing an acquaintance take the prize for the biggest pumpkin at the fair. I'm happy for her. I know that people's love for Duchess Goldblatt is real. But I can't feel it. It's not for me, you understand. I'm not loved the way Duchess is loved, and this confusion, this continually trying to integrate the two selves that exist in one being but have been received differently by the world, is part of what I tried to figure out in the book. I'm still trying to figure it out.

Are Motown bass lines the actual voices of the gods? I give you James Jamerson, isolated bass track, "What's Going On?"

— Mitchell Nobis, metro Detroit

If we think of the voice of God as self-assured, as reassuring, as deeply satisfying, as the essence of depth itself at play, then yes. I think it sounds exactly like Motown bass lines.

What is the most difficult aspect of omniscience?

— RM, New York City

The isolation, I suspect. Genius is isolating. I refer here not to myself, believe me — I am not a genius, despite what Duchess Goldblatt will tell you fifty million times—but I've observed this in the couple of bona fide geniuses I've known personally: how hard they work to maintain good relationships with others who see less, who understand less, whose minds are at work less fully. It's the idea of being too smart for your own good, the whispered warning: Hide your light. People won't like you if you stand out as too smart. I hope this idea is dying out, but I'm not sure. Some of the smartest people I know are the loneliest.

Michael tells Pentangeli that Roth tried to have Michael and his family killed; he tells Roth than Pentangeli is responsible. Is this good management, and what do their annual evaluations look like?

— Jon Danziger, New York

It's an excellent question; thank you. I was hoping someone would ask. Michael was drawing here on his deep understanding of Maslow's hierarchy of needs: Pentangeli is driven by a need for belongingness, love, and friendship; Roth is driven by the need for recognition and achievement. Using Maslow's motivational theory, Michael is able to produce a superior performance from them both short-term, but as for their annual evaluations: they're both dead, as it were, by the end of II. Possibly there's a case to be made that Michael's management style could benefit from an investigation into Herzberg's two-factor theory; we can certainly see evidence in I and II that his turnover costs are through the roof.

Questions for Discussion

1. What did you think about the way Anonymous interspersed Duchess's quotes throughout the book? Did you notice anything particular about placement? Which quotes were your favorite?

2. Anonymous follows several friendships throughout. Compare and contrast the relationships between those who knew Anonymous before, those who met Anonymous through Duchess, and folks who are friends with Duchess only. Duchess also has deep relationships with books and musicians. What do you think it meant for Anonymous to meet her own heroes?

3. The memoir starts with Anonymous reflecting on trauma: "The human mind is kind. It will create blank spaces for itself. I think of them as little airbags in my mind, cushioning the tender places where the blows and bruises are" (35). Discuss how the creation of the Duchess persona, and the online/real-life journey as Duchess seemed to

help Anonymous process her trauma. How would you describe the relationship between the Duchess and the narrator?

4. There are many moments of magic and serendipity throughout. Do you think these moments happen to everyone, or is there something special about Anonymous? Have you had similar moments in your own life?

5. "The damnedest thing was: she was better than me. I don't mean a better writer (although sometimes, yes, that too), but she was a better person. Duchess has perfect compassion and grace. My father was like that; he used to exhort me to have greater compassion, to find forgiveness, to love people more fully" (40–41). The narrator reflects on her father, and the loss of her father, throughout the memoir — yet she ultimately changes her mind about the correlation between her father and Duchess. Why do you think she does so? Who and what else influences Duchess's thoughts and tweets?

6. "She became a litmus test, if you will; if you liked Duchess's humor, and if you got her jokes and references, you'd probably like the other people who were drawn to her for the same reasons. Duchess's habit of responding to everyone who spoke to her was engendering the feeling of a welcoming, open-door salon in her timeline. It was organic. No one planned it. I certainly didn't plan it, nor could I have, any more than I could plan a successful party for a thousand strangers. It began to feel like a party to which everybody was invited" (58). What exactly about Anonymous and Duchess do you think helped create this

sense of community throughout Duchess's followers and fanbase?

7. "How do you make yourself a family out of thin air and good intentions?" (121). Throughout, Anonymous tells us the stories of her different families. What are the different types of families she brings up? What is her relationship to each?

8. What parallels did you see between Duchess and the narrator, conscious or subconscious?

9. "The more I've become Duchess and myself at once, both of us together with one voice, the more that my real tribe has been able to find me. Fancy that" (220). What do you think Anonymous means by this?

10. What do you think it means to be Goldblattian?